I Hate Red, You're Fired!

I Hate Red, You're Fired!

THE COLORFUL LIFE OF
AN INTERIOR DESIGNER

WILLIAM W. STUBBS

HARRY N. ABRAMS, INC., PUBLISHERS

Editor: Pamela Thomas
Designer: Helene Silverman
Production Manager: Justine Keefe

Photograph Credits: All photographs are from the author's private collection,
unless indicated otherwise below. Numbers refer to page numbers.

© Heike Bohnstengel: 87, 88, 89 (2 photos), 90, 91, 92, 93 (3 photos),
94, 95, 143. Courtesy Tyler London, Ltd.

© Chuck Choi: 123, 124.

© E. Joseph Deering: 15, 16, 17, 19, 142.

© Phillip H. Ennis: 2-3, 24, 25, 26 (2 photos), 27, 28, 30-31, 32, 33,
34 (1 photo), 35, 37, 40, 44 (1 photo), 45, 46-47, 48, 49, 50, 51, 52
(4 photos), 53, 54, 55, 56, 57 (2 photos), 58, 59, 60-61, 62, 63, 66,
67, 68-69, 70, 71, 142 (2 photos).

© Phyllis Hand : 8, 97.

© Heinz Kugler: jacket photographs, 10-11.

© Domonique Maurel: 8, 129.

© Rob Muir: 8, 76 (1 photo), 77, 78 (2 photos), 79, 99, 101, 102
(3 photos), 103, 104-105, 106, 107, 109, 111, 112, 113 (4 photos),
114-115, 116 (2 photos), 117, 118 (2 photos), 119 (2 photos), 120
(2 photos), 121 (2 photos), 142, 143 (4 photos).

© Aaron Usher III: 81, 82, 83, 142.

Library of Congress Cataloging-in-Publication Data

Stubbs, William W.
I hate red, you're fired! : the colorful life of an interior designer / by
William W. Stubbs.
p. cm.
Includes bibliographical references and index.
ISBN 0-8109-5577-6 (hardcover)
1. Stubbs, William W. 2. Interior decorators--United States--Biography.
I. Title.

NK2004.3.S78A2 2004
747'.092--dc22

2004012576

Printed and bound in China

10 9 8 7 6 5 4 3 2 1

Harry N. Abrams, Inc.
100 Fifth Avenue
New York, N.Y. 10011
www.abramsbooks.com

Abrams is a subsidiary of

LA MARTINIÈRE

To Shalle Cozac,
an extraordinary teacher who
inspires, motivates, encourages,
and befriends her students.
She planted seeds of possibility in me
when I badly needed focus and direction,
and, in so doing, she made all this possible.

And

To Dan Mysko,
my friend for more than 20 years
who thought he hated red, fired me,
and then ended up changing my life.

ACKNOWLEDGMENTS

MY LIFE's work is about meeting people's needs. When I work for a real estate developer who needs to sell or lease property, I use my skills to enhance the environment toward that goal. When I work for individuals, I am directed by their need for a home that serves their lifestyle, nurtures their innermost being, and lifts their spirits each time they walk in the door. I am motivated and inspired by stretching my abilities to meet—and hopefully exceed—the expectations of my clients.

I have never created in a vacuum, and I have been blessed with a large arsenal of creative people with whom I have collaborated. Looking at the beautiful pictures in this book, I see so much more than a finished interior: I see the meeting when I first talked about the space with my client; I see the plans on my desk as we brainstormed in the office; I see the meetings with contractors, painters, drapers, and others solving a multitude of problems; and I relive each highly charged installation day. I am grateful for the contributions of everyone involved in the evolution of these homes, buildings, and landscapes.

The homes in this book reflect the faith and confidence entrusted in me by many wonderful people. For starters, I want to thank Dan Mysko, my client and friend for more than 20 years, to whom this book, in part, is dedicated. The title, "I Hate Red, You're Fired!" is a direct quote from Dan, and most of the extreme experiences in my life I owe to him. Wonderful times I've enjoyed in Acapulco, Aspen, New York, London, Kiev, Moscow, Cannes, and so much more are due to Dan's generously including me in his extraordinary life.

My projects in the former Soviet Union could never have moved forward without the expertise and inexhaustible dedication of my friend, project director, architect, and translator in Kiev, Roman Shwed. I also want to thank David Canepari, Marc Plonskier, Jerri and Leroy Pesch, Judy and Paul Andrews, Sugar and Mike Barnes, Sueanne and Randy Nichols, and Carolyn Faulk for their generosity.

I am at my creative best because of my talented design partner, Dawn Frazier, who sees no problems—only solutions—and who, following a catastrophe, describes it as an adventure.

The loves of my life, Chad and Courtney Stubbs, and I share a light-hearted moment.

Among other dedicated and creative colleagues in my Houston office, I want to thank my ever-present, loving supporter, Agnes Sullivan; my wonderful implementer of ideas, Gwen Lawrence; and my sister, best friend and CPA, Sugar — God's gift to me.

The book could not have happened without my wonderful friend and writing partner, Madeleine McDermott Hamm.

I am truly grateful for Paige Rense and her incredible team at *Architectural Digest*, who have encouraged me not only by the great honor of including my work in their publication, but also by creating the highest standard for me as a designer.

I also want to thank Theo Kalomirakis, my mentor for this book, who has always been generous and a joy to work with; Claudia Landis, my first client and wonderful friend; and Carrye Crowder and all the great people at Robert Allen and Beacon Hill for their support.

My work and personal relationships have clearly been blessed by God, and through Him, I have enjoyed many gifts, including the friendship and advice of Tom Tewell, Dave Peterson, and Dave Carpenter.

All of this would lack so much without the loves of my life, Chad and Courtney Stubbs.

BILL STUBBS

Contents

Prologue

I MUST BE DREAMING

I SANK into seat 2A, Air France Flight 2945, Moscow to Paris. The wide first class seat seemed to wrap its arms around me and say, "There, there. It's going to be all right. You are safe in my arms." I immediately went into a deep sleep.

The last time I had slept was three days earlier at the Four Seasons Hotel in Beverly Hills. Could that be right? I had lost track of time and day. Yes, that's it, on Sunday night I was there in a suite with my daughter, sister, and mom.

Monday I flew to Houston. Tuesday I left for New York, then Paris and on to Moscow. Now it was Thursday morning, and I was on my way back to Paris, and the last time I had been in a bed was Sunday in that cloud of a heavenly bed at the Four Seasons.

"Monsieur Stubbs, Monsieur Stubbs!"

Oh, this was a good dream—the voice of a beautiful French woman calling my name.

"Monsieur Stubbs, Monsieur Stubbs!"

OK, it wasn't a dream. I was awakened from my deep sleep by the hand of the attractive flight attendant touching my shoulder.

"Monsieur Stubbs, you have business with zee pilot." I could not imagine what she was talking about. I thought I must still be asleep.

In a heavy French accent, she gently persisted.

"Monsieur Stubbs, you have business with zee pilot. Please stay in your seat until all zee passengers have left zee plane."

What was she talking about? I was totally confused, totally tired, so I took the path of least resistance and simply followed her orders. I stayed in my seat and waited for all the passengers to deplane. By the time everyone else had departed, I was a little more awake and sitting on the edge of my seat to see what on earth my business with "zee" pilot could be. I had just had a nightmarish experience in Moscow, but I thought all of that was behind me.

Next, to my surprise, two French policemen entered the plane and approached me. The pilot appeared behind them and handed them some kind of official-looking envelope, for which they signed. The envelope seemed to be related to me. It was.

I WAS BEING ARRESTED BY THE FRENCH POLICE!

By now, I was wide awake. In fact, it was as if someone had thrown a pitcher of ice water in my face.

As I silently walked between the two officers, my mind raced to find some explanation for these extreme events. I was, it seemed to me, an unlikely person to be in this predicament. If asked, I would define myself as a dad, a Sunday School teacher, and an interior designer—not much of a threat to the French Government.

What road had led me to this place? At which fork had I taken the wrong turn? Where did it all start?

Was it at the Cannes Film Festival a few months earlier when I met the muscle-bound Ukrainian restaurateur wearing a skimpy Speedo? Was it the time years before that when I had flown to the Ukraine and was escorted off the plane by KGB officers? Or was it even earlier than that, when I had done a job in Switzerland? No, I think it was that guidance counselor at El Campo High School who said, "Bill, with your grades, you should consider going into air-conditioning repair."

I have been running from that suggestion for thirty years.

The interior design profession is so civilized, so glamorous, so safe. . .or so everyone thinks. Apparently, when most people consider the life of an interior designer, they envision elegant rooms filled with luxurious fabrics and exotic woods, silver candlesticks and fresh flowers in crystal vases, and happy clients sipping champagne and toasting their designer.

Or so some designers would have you believe.

But not me.

If you think joining the CIA or becoming a mountain climber promises adventure, let me introduce you to my entree to an exciting life—decorating. Being an interior designer has its ups and downs, but for me, in recent years, it's been mainly takeoffs and landings as I have jetted to fascinating, and often unpredictable, jobs in far-flung places—from Acapulco and Newport to Kiev and now Moscow.

As a kid in the little town of El Campo, Texas, I was always interested in design and the way things looked, so, despite my guidance counselor's advice, I decided to enroll at the International Institute of Design in Washington, D.C. I have found myself dealing with a lot more than floor plans and faux finishes since graduating from design school and heading to Houston, ready to redecorate the world.

Although I have developed strong ideas about design over the years, I take a holistic approach to each project, considering every aspect, from the site and architecture of the building or space to the tastes and dreams of my clients. I like to personalize every space I decorate. My goal is always to have the client say, "This is me!"

But at times I've had to take some pretty big risks to reach these goals.

A pivotal point came in 1981, the first time I was fired by a client I still work with to this day, an oil trader originally from the Ukraine. He's a technical kind of guy. He has to see a space entirely completed to decide whether or not he likes it. He can't envision it.

I was decorating his new penthouse condominium in an exclusive high rise in Houston called The Houstonian, and using a lot of red. My client's assistant was keeping an eye on me and reporting my every move back to her boss. While my client was on a trip to Brazil, he walked into a dining room he did not like. It was red, so he instantly decided he did not like red.

He called me from Brazil and said, "I saw a red room today. I hated it. I hate red. You're fired!"

At that moment, I was standing in his living room, with one hundred yards of red custom-dyed Brunschwig & Fils fabric, unrolled, and ready to go on the walls.

"Well, now you own a hundred yards of red fabric," I said to him. "What would you like me to do with it?"

We won't say what he told me to do with that fabric.

So I made a decision—which turned out to be not only correct, but a critical turning point in my career: I decided to go ahead and finish the room, fired or not. Everything was there, ready to go, so we finished it before he returned from Brazil.

You can probably predict how this all turned out. He loved it! He also fell in love with the color red, and now he wants it in every room, in every place we do together—and we have done many over the past 20 years. In fact, it's a battle when I want to use another color.

But, back to those Parisian policemen escorting me off that plane. Don't worry. I will finish that story. But first, let me take you on a few other flights to destinations filled with adventures that ultimately will bring us back to that one particular flight from Moscow to Paris.

1 The Houston Penthouse

WRAPPED IN RED

opposite: To set the stage for the dramatic design throughout the penthouse, an opulent gilt console purchased in London stands out against the rich red wall. The mirrored ceiling with brass moldings creates an illusion of grander dimensions in the entry.

THERE WERE many pinch pleats, recliners, and laminate countertops between my arrival in Houston in the early 1970s and that first challenging penthouse assignment. Any young designer has to pay his dues, and in Houston in the 1970s, the best places to gain experience, and hopefully clients, were the design studios of several large furniture and department stores. I was one of a stable of young, talented designers who landed at Foley's department store under the inspiring leadership of T. Miles Gray, who had been lured from New York to establish a design beachhead in the Texas boomtown.

At Foley's, I began to realize that a significant part of being an interior designer was helping people select recliners. Frankly, after a few months, I thought I would just have to shoot myself if pairing lounge chairs with clients was going to be the defining aspect of my career. I decided I had to go in another direction.

So, after only one year at Foley's, I started my own interior design firm. Most of my work was with various developers building apartment complexes around Houston, the state of Texas, and along the Eastern seaboard. I would decide whether the doorknobs should be shiny brass, antique brass, or chrome, and if the carpet should be beige, beiger, or very beige. If the kitchen appliances were white, what color the laminate on the kitchen counters should be—decisions like that. Granted, this wasn't the glamorous world of interior design I was seeking, but it beat choosing recliners.

Then, in the early 1980s, I got a call from the developers of The Houstonian, a brand-new, luxury high-rise condominium, and, from that moment on, everything changed. The people buying these apartments wanted a serious interior designer, and suddenly I was working for clients who did not want just a recliner or wall-to-wall beige carpeting. They wanted sophisticated wall coverings, custom-made furniture, and antiques. This was more like it!

My first big job for a wealthy client was the Ukrainian oil trader's penthouse. This guy had just gotten a divorce, and all he had was his luggage. I checked out the luggage, trying to determine if his style was contemporary, traditional, or something else. Later he told me he hadn't bought the luggage; his ex-wife had, which was not much of an indicator of his style preference.

opposite: The turn-of-the-century Russian bronze in the foreground speaks to the client's Eastern European heritage. Intricate ormulu embellishes the handsome French commode in the background.
left: The bar, defined by a bold counter crafted of red antique marble inset with brass trim, adds a sleek, contemporary touch to this bachelor's penthouse.

Fortunately for me, this client was relying on me to create a persona for him through the look of his penthouse interiors. Because he was constantly traveling, the client frequently sent his administrative assistant to check on the project's progress. Then he would call me from some far off location and scream, "I know what you're doing up there!" Eventually, I realized that he was just letting me know that he was on top of things. The assistant had told him we were painting or installing lighting, or whatever we were doing that day. The client was not complaining; he was just letting me know that he was in control.

But the day he called from Brazil was different. He was very angry. This time I knew he actually *was* complaining. He knew we were designing his penthouse around the color red,

opposite: The deep red, custom-dyed Brunschwig & Fils herringbone cotton chenille that covers the living room walls is the very fabric the client was certain he would hate, but ultimately loved. A pair of bergeres upholstered in white wool flecked with gold contrast with the red walls and red oversized sofas. The magnificent 14-by-22-foot Bijar carpet provides a colorful, yet traditional, anchor to the large, open space.

which, to me, somehow spoke to his Eastern European background. But he had seen a red dining room in Brazil and he absolutely loathed it. Suddenly, he hated red, and I was fired.

However, not only did I have one hundred yards of very expensive, red Brunschwig & Fils fabric from France rolled out in front of me, ready for installation, I had two custom-made red sofas on the way. Unfortunately, the client was on his way, too.

I decided to take a risk—to barge ahead and finish the job. I had a feeling once he saw it, he would love it.

The sofas arrived, but as luck would have it, they would not fit into the elevator, even when part of the roof was removed. I told the delivery men that they had to get those sofas to the 21st floor, and soon! Reluctantly, they started to carry one of the sofas up the stairs, but it wouldn't go around the corner. I considered sawing them in half, but wondered if we'd ever be able to glue them back together. I even inquired about using a crane, but discovered it wouldn't reach that high, and besides, would require special city permits. Plus, I would probably have to break out a window. Too complicated.

Finally, I called the Otis Elevator Company. They suggested that we put the sofas on top of the elevator.

"Who exactly should do that?" I asked. "Not the designer, I hope."

So Otis sent three men and, along with the furniture movers, they managed to put each 9-foot-long sofa on top of the elevator—holding it upright—and slowly brought it up 21 floors. It worked. I couldn't believe it.

I worked day and night to finish the whole apartment. I wanted it to be perfect when my client arrived, with music playing, the candles lit, and fresh flowers everywhere. I kept thinking, "Maybe he won't notice the red." I decided I would turn the lights down low so he would focus on his beautiful view, while the red walls and sofas would simply provide a warm glow.

When he walked in, he looked around and started applauding. This guy actually applauded! He loved it!

That was more than 20 years ago and, since then, I have designed three additional residences for him. And we still battle about red. It seems I created a monster. Now, all he wants is red!

The Ukrainian Cottage

A GEM IN THE WOODS

MY CLIENT, the oil trader with the penthouse in Houston, wanted to return to his roots in the Ukraine, the country his family had fled after World War II. In 1994, he acquired a 20-acre estate outside of Kiev and sent for me to turn it into a showplace. That was the beginning of a four-year odyssey that would take me to the Ukraine once every eight weeks for a stay of about 10 days each time. During these years, I experienced not only every conceivable kind of weather and travel problem, but every dilemma a designer could imagine—and some I could never have imagined.

The first time I visited, which was about three years after the fall of the former Soviet Union, I flew from Houston to Amsterdam, then on to Kiev. The flight on KLM was very civilized, but still I couldn't help feeling apprehensive.

When we landed, I looked out the window, and everything was snowy and bleak—like the way you'd imagine Siberia. Then the airplane door opened, and two large men came on board wearing long, heavy, woolen military coats and sable hats, and carrying big machine guns! Actually, I don't know anything about guns, but they looked like machine guns to me.

The two men made an announcement in a language that I could not understand. Then they conferred with the flight attendant, who wrote "Will Mr. Stubbs please ring his call button?" on a piece of paper and held it up for the passengers to see.

Once I identified myself, these two guys escorted me off the plane and into a little car that looked like an old Nash Rambler—except the seats were covered in slipcovers my mother might have made. (By the way, my mother doesn't sew.) They placed me in the back seat of this cramped car between two more men in big coats and sable hats (and carrying guns) and we drove off. I was terrified, but after a long, tense drive, we pulled up in front of what I subsequently learned was the finest hotel in Kiev.

That was my introduction to the former Soviet Union. I later learned from my client that I had received "the royal treatment!" (Who would have guessed? It's very funny how "the royal treatment" and "being arrested" seemed very similar.) My "greeters" turned out to be former KGB agents who were now in special service for the Ukrainian president. That boxy, gray, vintage car was an official government vehicle called a Lada.

The hotel had a huge four-story lobby that was all marble, with an enormous contemporary-looking light fixture ("chandelier" seems too grand a word) hanging in the middle. I was thinking this wouldn't be so bad.

I checked in and got a key to my room. No one offered to help with my luggage. The elevator was big enough for only me and my bags. When the elevator door opened on my floor, the hallway was almost dark. There were light fixtures, but no lights were turned on.

A small, square woman was sitting in the hallway, holding a book. She didn't speak, but she watched as I walked down the hall, and she made a little note in the book. She was

below left: The modern appearance of the exterior of the Hotel Natsionalny in Kiev belies what I found inside. To an interior designer from the United States, this "first class" hotel proved more than austere, it was creepy.

always there, day or night, for the entire time I stayed at the hotel, but I never learned why she was stationed in the hall or what the marks in her book meant.

Up to this point, the hotel had seemed like a bad imitation of a Hyatt Regency. Any similarity to a fine hotel ended the moment I opened the door to my room. The word "cell" crossed my mind—it was very basic, like a monk's room in a monastery—although the space didn't really seem to be a place that would stimulate profound introspection. Two narrow beds with two-inch-thick pads on top of plywood bases were shoved against the walls. The window was frosted over, reminding me of those wintry scenes from the movie *Doctor Zhivago*.

Being an American, I am accustomed to commercialism or "branding." When you check into a hotel, its name is on everything—the welcome mat, the towels, the soap, and, of course, all the printed materials. I couldn't find a name anywhere in this hotel. The absence of any acknowledgment of the hotel's name was unnerving.

above center and right: The typical Ukrainian bed was less than 36 inches wide, with a pad (forget a mattress) about two inches thick and sheets that gave me a rash. In the early days of working on the Ukrainian estate, I had to stay in this hotel about 10 days per trip. My nights here prompted me to finish the little guest cottage as quickly as possible.

When I first encountered the caretaker's cottage, I could not imagine a more humble, or less attractive, dwelling. It had low ceilings, tiny rooms, an uneven floor, and a bathroom so primitive that it was hardly usable. It was no wonder my client saw no possibility for reclaiming this simple structure.

So, feeling anxious to learn the hotel's name, I left the room, passed the woman sitting in the hall—who made a check mark in her book—and made my way out of the building. I could not find the hotel's name anywhere—not on the door, not on a sign, not even on a doormat. By this time it was getting dark, and I noticed there were no street lights, no signs for restaurants, nothing. I longed to see some Golden Arches!

When I went back inside, I was amazed to discover that the three-story-high chandelier in the lobby had only one incandescent light bulb—probably about 60 watts—burning in its center. With that one light on, I could see that the fixture that had originally looked to me like a staggered glass design now appeared to be made of little jelly jars. The only other light in the lobby came from a black-and-white television screen. Some guards were watching a comedy show, their faces lit by the glow of the TV. It was creepy.

When my client showed up, I learned I was staying in Hotel Natsionalny, which is owned by the Ukrainian government. He also informed me that visitors had to pay in cash (preferably brand new American $100 bills) for everything, and would not get a receipt. I could not use credit cards or even old, wrinkled American dollars; however, since I hadn't been told about any of this, my client took care of everything.

Not only did I find that things were very expensive in Kiev, but that goods and services could have two prices—a high price for foreigners and a more reasonable price for local residents. You could change money for local currency at little kiosks on the street, but it took satchels full of that currency to pay for anything.

By the way, Kiev is not far from Chernobyl, the place that experienced the hideous nuclear meltdown in 1986. After the nuclear accident, the city of Kiev was wrapped in a cloud of radiation, and many considered it to be the most polluted city in the world. This was definitely a concern for me. In fact, one of the first things I did when we started the project was take soil samples and send them to Munich to be tested for radiation, because I wasn't sure I wanted to hang around there if the ground was seriously contaminated. It wasn't.

My client's new estate had belonged to a former Soviet official who was ousted after the accident at Chernobyl. The large main house had been vacant since then, watched over only by a caretaker and a housekeeper. When I arrived there in 1994, the mansion had been vacant for nearly a decade. It was so eerie, because it looked like someone had left only minutes before. The beds were made; the linens were perfect. There wasn't a speck of dust anywhere. Still, although this had been a grand house during the Soviet regime, it was drab and depressing, totally lacking in any warmth or beauty.

As my client and I inspected the 20-acre estate, I felt overwhelmed. We walked around the property and came upon a little caretaker's cottage. The idea of a "caretaker's cottage" sounds romantic, but, believe me, this place wasn't a cute little fairy-tale house, unless you wanted to apply the word "grim." It was a rickety thing with little bitty rooms, tiny doors, and nothing more than a freestanding sink and a little gas cooker in the kitchen. It was even more depressing than the big house.

My client declared that we should just tear the cottage down. However, I was beginning to think this whole project was so daunting that perhaps we should start with remodeling something small, like this little building. It could have a beginning and an end—or, at least I could imagine an end.

It also occurred to me that perhaps I could turn the cottage into a place where I could stay as I worked on the mansion. I was staying in the finest hotel in the Ukraine, but I had a rash from the scratchy sheets. I needed something more comfortable.

So I said, "Why don't we remodel this as a guest cottage?"

He, of course, said "No."

"We really need something we can complete," I insisted. "I'm a completion kind of person. Also, we will need a place to operate from, a central location. I need a place to have a computer, a fax machine, a satellite dish—things like that."

My client was absolutely against remodeling the cottage until the day it was finished. Then he fell in love with it and even hosted the Ukrainian president in his elegant little cottage in the forest.

But, in the beginning, it was like reinventing the wheel. Renovating the caretaker's cottage turned out to be an experiment for the entire project. We learned so much.

The many roadblocks we encountered stemmed from the poor quality of locally available construction materials and the lack of up-to-date tools and technology. Plus, the workers were unfamiliar with methods and materials we expected to use. However, they adapted quickly to

the equipment and products we brought in from the west. Also, at that time, the Ukrainian currency was temporary and could not be exchanged outside that country. Everything was very complicated.

I ended up having to travel all over Europe looking for sources. I bought very modern kitchen appliances in Germany, light fixtures in Prague, furniture in Milan, antiques in Paris, and rugs in London. But, it became very time-consuming and difficult. Everything arrived in dribs and drabs, required expensive duty, and had to be guarded and protected until it could be installed. Ultimately, through trial and error, I realized that assembling everything in the United States and sending it in one shipment was the most efficient way to operate.

Also, we wanted to use local labor, and that was another learning experience. When I began to interview contractors and workmen, I realized that it had been five or six generations since a truly nice house had been built in the Ukraine. They had no frame of reference for what a luxurious residence would be like. Everything had been done with a "central committee/ communist/socialist" kind of attitude. For example, if you were a married couple with two children, you were allotted so many square feet of space. They had no sense that anything else was even possible.

With the local workmen, I faced a barrier of understanding as well as of language. To them, things that were luxurious were usually Western, and always brand spanking new. That was the ultimate achievement—to own something new. They also liked to see all the latest technology—

opposite: Layers of textures, patterns, and rich colors create a special sense of warmth and grandeur in the cottage's tiny living room. By taking out the attic and arranging art and other objects high on the wall, the space feels larger, although the room's dimensions have not changed.
above: Recalling the many hours I spent eating or working at this dining table, I felt that I could have lived in this space indefinitely. The peace and tranquility present in this jewel box create an overall sense of well-being.

above: No matter how frigid and foreboding the outside world might be—and there were many days like that—the master bedroom gave me a warm, soothing feeling whenever I stepped into it.

right: This opulent bed in the master bedroom caused quite a stir among the local residents.

the wide-screen TVs, the big speakers, the CD players—which is also a European way of doing interiors. On the other hand, I wanted all the technology to disappear into the background.

I wanted to create a patina of late 19th-, early 20th-century Europe. The workmen did exquisite woodwork but had a hard time understanding that when it was finished, it had to be distressed and stained. So, I had to fight at every corner. However, like my client, in the end they were amazed. The workmen were proud of what they had done, and said, "Now we understand; we know why you wanted it to be this way."

Having always been enamored with the early 20th-century Czarist period, the age of Nicholas and Alexandra, I wanted to research what the Ukraine had been like prior to the Russian Revolution and to bring the feeling of that period into the cottage as well as the large house. I really wanted to create something that had some sense of history to it, as well as flavor and eclecticism. This was especially true since my client, who had been born in the Ukraine prior to World War II and had lost everything when his family escaped, wanted this house to re-create some of his lost heritage.

Which brings me to the story of the bed.

To understand about the bed, you have to first know about beds in the Ukraine. First, like the beds in the hotel, all beds are single size, maybe less than 36-inches wide, with a plywood base, and a two-inch-thick pad (not a mattress) on top. Then, a sheet is put over this futon-type pad, and the sheet is topped with a casing that looks like a big pillowcase (not a duvet cover),

The second bedroom, though somewhat smaller than the master bedroom, was no less luxurious. The rich, warm colors coupled with the collection of paintings by local artists add to the room's comfort and charm. The artwork was found in local open markets and galleries.

Only rarely did I have time to enjoy a cup of tea on the little terrace outside the cottage. The beautiful furniture was carved by a local artisan. I would show him pictures of what I envisioned, and the completed furniture would be waiting on my next visit.

and that encases a nasty-looking horsehair blanket. The pillows are big and square, and the sheets are made of such rough fabric that they practically give you a rug burn.

Every bed I'd seen in the Ukraine was simply awful — even the beds in the best hotel. So I set out to assemble a luxurious bed for the little cottage, and it ended up becoming a thing of wonder to the local residents. People came from miles around to see this thick, pillow-top, queen-size mattress and box springs. They watched me add two dust ruffles, a mattress pad, a layer of fleece, soft, fine sheets, a fluffy duvet, and nine pillows. They were absolutely fascinated.

What I found particularly nice was that no one resented any of this excess. They were excited to learn about different ways of doing things. Anytime I would do anything new, the housekeepers would come after me, and I would hear them saying in Ukrainian, "Bill's going to do something." They wanted to watch and learn exactly how to do it, too.

One of the most memorable moments I had in the little cottage had nothing to do with remodeling or decorating. I had pictured this place as a little Hansel-and-Gretel cottage with window boxes and shutters that could actually be pulled closed. So that's what we had made, and that solved the problem of having fancy draperies and not being able to take down the tiebacks and close them.

Every night at dusk, the guards on the property would come by and close the shutters. However, I didn't like it because I would feel trapped the next morning and couldn't open the shutters from the inside. So, I told the guards to stop closing the shutters. I figured it was enough that I was on this estate behind huge, high walls with two guards that checked on me several times during the night. I just left the windows uncovered in order to get the morning sunlight.

One morning about two o'clock as I was sleeping in my heavenly bed, I was awakened by what sounded like an explosion, followed by a loud commotion and barking. I looked out a window to see a line of military people with flashlights and angry dogs approaching my little cottage. This was also around the time that American businessmen were often being kidnapped in Moscow, and many people thought the Ukraine was equally dangerous. But I'd been working there for over a year, so I felt perfectly secure in my little world.

Suddenly, uniformed men with guns and dogs had surrounded the cottage and were banging on the front door and screaming in Russian. I opened the door to see these loud, burly military men with Uzis and barking dogs, and I had no idea what was going on. My first thought was that these were just kids, 18- and 19-year-old boys. My second thought was they were not much different from a gang. And they didn't speak English.

I could see one of the estate's guards standing behind the crowd, looking very helpless because the situation was completely out of his control. However, evidently I was so non-threatening standing there in my underwear that I didn't need to speak their language to explain that I was no danger to anyone. They looked at me, up and down, and turned around and left. Quite humiliating, as I look back.

Hours later, after the translator arrived, I learned what had happened. The head of the Ukrainian parliament lived on the adjoining estate, and someone had tried to assassinate him. A car bomb had been planted to go off the next morning when he was to leave for work, but it had exploded early. The soldiers were frantically searching, guns ready, for the person who had placed the bomb.

Apparently, they could tell in an instant that I couldn't be the bomber.

below: I could hardly contain my excitement after completing this precious cottage, which would serve as my home-away-from-home for years as I worked on other buildings and the grounds of the estate.

overleaf: The cottage, located in the middle of a dense forest, turned out to be as glorious a getaway in the summer as it was a warm, cozy retreat in the dead of winter.

The Dacha

SPLENDOR IN THE UKRAINE

above: The gazebo is mirrored in the lake.
opposite: The graceful staircase in the main house replaced the original straight, practical—and very awkward—stairs. It had to be torn out and rebuilt three times in order to achieve the correct balance and aesthetics.

THE moment I saw my client's estate in the Ukraine, I was overwhelmed. First of all, he had purchased 20 acres of uncultivated, unlandscaped property with a rectangular, man-made lake. The main house was austere and ungainly, the caretaker's cottage was virtually falling down, and there were several other outer buildings not immediately evident to us.

My first impulse, which ultimately proved beneficial to everyone concerned, was to renovate the ramshackle caretaker's cottage. That took about a year. (The details of that renovation are described in Chapter 2.) My client was thrilled with the results, and I must say, so was I. Plus, by starting with a much smaller building, we learned a tremendous amount about how we would have to work in modern-day Ukraine.

To find craftsmen, I visited museums, theaters, and other local buildings, and when I saw work I admired, I asked who did it. Through this sort of word-of-mouth effort, we discovered local artisans who could do amazing things. The plasterers could sculpt anything I could dream up. The woodworkers, stonemasons, and carpenters were more than craftsmen — they were artists. And because of the economy in post-Soviet Ukraine, they all needed the work.

We worked on the houses and the property the way I imagined architects and designers worked more than 100 years ago on the big houses in Europe and even in America, when people such as the Vanderbilts were building grand estates and establishing their heritage. Back then, there were no Home Depots and all the sources we have today. Everything had to be created, and that's what we did in Kiev. Workers renovated and expanded the main house and transformed the property into a park-like setting. New and antique furnishings from around the world were selected, and at the same time, the house was given state-of-the-art European and American appliances and technology. It was an exhilarating experience.

right: Inside the charming boyhood home, furnishings and objects reflect the way people lived in this part of the world long ago.
opposite: The re-created boyhood home of the client was constructed using methods dating back hundreds of years, and became one of my favorite parts of the complex residential project.
below: Our contractor, Volodio, and I tour the historic Ukrainian villages.

THE BOYHOOD HOME

Today's bustling Kiev is quite different from the bleak city I first encountered in 1994. There was nothing to do—and I mean nothing. The only thing my client could think of for us to do was visit a farm where they demonstrated how local people lived in past times. It was like the Ukraine's answer to historic Natchez or Colonial Williamsburg, but on a very modest scale. During our visit, my client pointed at a little mud hut and said, "This is like the place where I was born."

As a joke, I said: "Why don't we put a replica of your boyhood home on your property? We'll have places on the estate that people can visit, and one of the stops will be your boyhood home."

I was kidding, but my client got excited, clapped his hands, and said: "Do it!"

My joke changed the course of the whole Kiev project. No longer was I just renovating a mansion and a guest cottage and planting a few shrubs. I was creating a private world for my client, almost a small Ukrainian theme park with different buildings to visit and unexpected vistas, each with a distinct personality. This was quickly turning into a project unlike any other I had ever tackled.

I re-created his boyhood home from scratch. He had nothing from his childhood, since his family fled the Ukraine with only a suitcase. We collected vintage furnishings that looked like pieces he remembered. I decorated the little house like a classic peasant cottage. Curiously, the people working on the property would bring little things they had at home, which I thought was a lovely gesture. For the finishing touch, we planted a summer garden in front of the house with humble sunflowers and poppies. It was like a little museum, a lovely place to look at, nothing else.

THE PARK

above: After creating an island in the lake, I wanted to build a Monet-type bridge, and a picturesque gazebo.

top: Standing on the unpainted bridge, I found the natural beauty of the setting tranquil and almost mesmerizing.

When I first arrived, the closest thing to a redeeming landscape feature on the property was a lake, which was actually a large, man-made pond that looked like a tank on a Texas farm. I decided to make it look like a pond in one of Monet's water lily paintings, including an island with a gazebo and a charming little bridge to reach it.

To achieve this vision, we first drained the lake. Then I stood in what would ultimately be the middle of the lake and plotted out the island so it would catch beautiful light and reflect the gazebo in the water.

In addition, I wanted another bridge, but made of stone and similar in style to the bridges Frederick Law Olmsted and Calvert Vaux designed for Central Park in New York. No water existed naturally where I planned the stone bridge, so we redirected the lake to make it flow

under the new bridge. Today, grass grows right up to the lake's edge, and it looks like it is fed from a nearby spring.

After the lake and the stone bridge were finished, I decided it still needed something more — specifically, a waterfall. We planned the waterfall so that it "fell" at the back of the lake, where it would look like a natural part of the surroundings. A stepped concrete structure was built to direct the falling water, then blended into the surroundings, rock-by-rock and plant-by-plant. Finally, we laid a path of large stepping stones at the foot of the waterfall. Eventually moss covered the rocks and stones.

I wanted the grounds to look as if everything had been there for a hundred years — one of the concepts the Ukrainian workers had difficulty grasping. Why make something look old? They valued the "new." But in the end, they appreciated the beauty we created.

above: The gazebo was positioned in the middle of the island so that it would reflect beautifully in the lake. For me, the whole effect of the gazebo, the bridge, and the lake took on a magical quality, like something in a painting.

Although the addition of a waterfall became a huge engineering and construction feat, the final result justified the effort. The stepped concrete structure that directs the water flow is disguised by rocks, plants, and moss.

above: My dream to build a bridge similar to those that Calvert Vaux designed 150 years ago in New York's Central Park came to reality due to the genius of the local stonemasons, here at work on the bridge.

left: The workmen were puzzled that I wanted the stone bridge to look old; however, when it was finished and they saw how beautifully it blended into the landscape, they understood completely.

overleaf: The completed stone bridge and walkway seemed to settle into the landscape and look as if they had always been there.

above: Built in the early 1950s for a high-ranking Soviet official, the main house was structurally solid, but architecturally awkward, at least to my taste. *below*: After the renovation and expansion, the handsome house retained many of its original design elements but had evolved into a more graceful and grand residence.

THE MAIN HOUSE

The residence, which had been the dacha of a high-ranking Soviet official, had been built in the 1950s by Polish prisoners of war, and it looked it. By definition, a dacha is a grand Russian country house or cottage, but this place would not even come close to meeting Western expectations for a fine home.

Determining the destiny of the main house brought on another battle with my client. He had decided it wasn't large enough and wanted to demolish it and start over. Although I did not think it was an attractive house, I was determined to remodel it. Saving the original structure gave the whole plan greater integrity. The house was considered the finest in the country, and my client was encountering considerable outside opposition to tearing it down.

So we kept the house and added an entirely new section that encompasses the main living room and the grand, state-of-the-art theater. Eventually the house would contain approximately 6,500 square feet of space.

left: To fulfill my client's wish for a red bar in the entrance hall, I hid it behind a counter-weighted mirror that disappears into the basement with the touch of a finger, revealing the red, jewel box-like bar. The bookcase is actually the door to the bar.

overleaf: Draped with pale salmon Schumacher silk on the windows and walls and topped with the quatrefoil-patterned plaster ceiling, the morning room glows in the early hours of sunlight.

My client and I had yet another battle—one of many, actually—concerning the entrance hall. I had painted the entry white. He said it looked "unfinished" and added, "It's not cheery. I want red." To complicate matters, he also wanted a bar in the entryway—a long, sweeping bar with barstools. I said it would look like a brothel with red walls and a bar. But he insisted.

I told him I'd give him a bar and he'd love it, but I couldn't do it his way. He didn't agree; he never does. But I went ahead, and created an illusion. I kept the main foyer an elegant and dignified white, and I installed a bookcase that was also a door that swung open to a small, jewel box-like bar. Against an adjoining wall, above a console table, I hung a counter-weighted mirror that lowers into the basement with the touch of a finger, revealing the bar, which is red, of course. It's all quite startling and effective. And, naturally, my client loved surprising guests with his secret bar.

Rich shades of red were used throughout the house, including in the living room, dining room, master bedroom, and even in the very modern kitchen. But I rebelled, again, against red for the morning room, which might also be called the breakfast room. I treated this space to a delicate, pale salmon silk from Schumacher, accented with elegant passementerie. I told my client "You don't want a red room in the morning." He hated it and called it a "sissy room."

Another place I passed on red was the large guest room. I thought it should be peaceful and quietly elegant, so it's layered in shades of ecru and white.

The second guest room became a little jewel — and ultimately one of my favorite rooms — even though the owner thought it was too small to be a bedroom. It's a wonderful, busy little bedroom with Scalamandré silk on the walls and Brunschwig & Fils silk on the bed. I had the craftsmen copy the design of the Chinese rug we used on the floor onto the ceiling. They did it all in plaster.

I told my client I was going to turn a little niche off that bedroom into a bathroom, and, again, he said it was too small. But I did it anyway, and it has this great Old World feeling and looks as if it was in the house originally. Lovely, etched glass French doors separate the bath from the bedroom.

opposite: The elaborate powder room was inspired by my discovery of the luxury wall–covering firm, Zuber Cie, on a back street in Paris. The black-lacquered paper creates an opulent background for the antique gilt mirror found in an antiques shop in Kiev.
left: Because the first guest room was part of the addition, it could be sized generously, with a gracious space for reading, relaxing, and late-night dining. Furnishings were selected for comfort first, then for the sumptuous textures and patterns in the textiles.

overleaf left: The first guest room was part of a brand new addition to the original house, yet, in part because of the beautiful molding, it looks as if it has been there for centuries.
overleaf right: The white and ecru palette of the guest room ended up being my favorite color scheme in the entire house. And, although I never slept in it, I thought this was the most inviting bed I had ever designed.

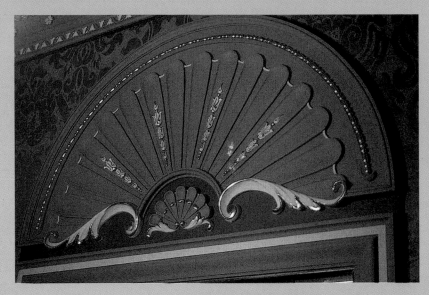

above: Decorative detailing of the guest bath shows off the talent of the local plaster artisans and painters contributing to the Kiev project.
near right: A nautical niche in the foyer to the guest bath holds a delicate reproduction of "The Three Graces."
far right, top: From polished marble to an intricate bronze grill to silk brocade, the decorative elements of the guest bath blend into a visual feast.
far right, below: Intricate detail upon rich detail adds to the layers of luxe in the guest bath.

opposite: The jewel-like guest bath is actually as practical as it is luxurious. It meets my belief that symmetry is the quickest path to the appearance of grandeur.

above: As with all the bedrooms on the estate, I insisted that the second guest room have a marvelously sumptuous bed. I remember waking up on many nights thinking of details I wanted to incorporate into this little cocoon of color and pattern.
opposite: Even though my client considered the space too small, I was able to turn this tiny second guest room into a gem, or what I like to call "an 'aha!' moment."

opposite: A tiny alcove off the equally tiny bedroom was transformed into a charming bathroom. French doors with etched glass panels separate the rooms.

above: Handmade tiles and a footed bathtub give the illusion of age and patina in the alcove-turned-bath.

left: The only place the sink could be positioned was under the window, but it conveys a wonderful Old World feeling.

left: My inspiration for the living room ceiling came from an Hermès scarf I had once watched a woman wrap seductively around her neck. The red fabric on the walls is reminiscent of the fabric I originally used in the owner's Houston penthouse, and the large Bijar rug also came from that same apartment.

previous pages, left: The gilt console at left was originally purchased for the client's penthouse in Houston. Icons are a very special part of the Ukrainian Orthodox Church; this is a beautiful example.
previous pages, right: In the master bedroom, the mahogany four-poster bed is fit for a king, with its oxblood silk spread and hangings embellished with the Napoleonic bee motif and gold braid trim.

61

opposite: Over-the-top opulence, created by the ceiling mural, the window treatments, and the painted plaster molding, makes the dining room formal enough for state dinners. *above*: Fine wood proved difficult to obtain in the Ukraine, so for a clubby wood-paneled look in the study, plasterwork was faux finished to look like wood.

right: The local artisans never ceased to amaze me. Any detail I could imagine could be turned into reality by a sculptor or craftsman. This plaster is ready to be sculpted by glass transfer.
below: The artisans painstakingly work on plaster casts, molding details in the same way it was done for the Czars.

64

left, top: Hand-carved plaster molding for the wall and ceiling is processed, start to finish, in the same room where it is ultimately installed.

above: Plaster molding is preferable to wood because it is more flexible, and also because artisans can produce it on site in just a few days.

left: This ceiling molding, completed and ready for painting, is absolutely beautiful in its unpainted, bisque state.

THE LOG PLAYHOUSE

My client continued to worry about not having enough space, so I suggested that we build a party pavilion. On a trip to Helsinki, I found an interesting log house that would be perfect. It was dismantled, shipped to Kiev and rebuilt on the estate by Finnish laborers trained to put it back together.

It's a large, lodge-like structure designed only as a party house. There are no bedrooms or formal entertaining rooms. The grand room features an antler chandelier, a jukebox, a pool table, a dining area, and a kitchen. There's a loft with exercise equipment equal to the best health clubs, and the area below the loft contains saunas, a steam room, a Jacuzzi, a massage room, and several showers. An entire football team could work out there. The tennis courts are located close by. My client had entertained frequently in the guest cottage, but from the moment the log house was completed, it became his favorite place for casual parties.

The lodge-like log house, found in Helsinki, dismantled and reassembled on the grounds of the estate, became a popular party pavilion.

THE WINE CELLAR

At some point, we discovered this little hump in the ground that turned out to be an old bomb shelter. We transformed it into the most charming wine cellar — another destination for visitors. My client had read in a wine connoisseur magazine that a genuine wine cellar must have at least 2,000 bottles on the racks, so he began buying wine like there was no tomorrow. I backlit all the racks so light comes through the bottles for an interesting effect.

Wine, however, is not the drink of choice in Kiev. It's vodka. And there's this strong male camaraderie atmosphere over there. At times I felt a little bit like a frontiersman. You'd go out to dinner, and before you knew it, there would be 12 people at your table — ex-patriots and others eager for conversation. The custom was to toast each person at the table. That would mean 12 shots of vodka before dinner arrived. Since I quit drinking years before, I would toss the vodka over my shoulder as the others drained their glasses. After several shots, nobody would notice or care what I was doing.

From time to time, visiting design specialists from the United States would be subjected to the vodka toasting at dinner. Later, most would confess to me how terrible they felt the next day. "How do you do it?" they would ask, only then to learn my secret over-the-shoulder strategy.

A hump we discovered in the landscape turned out to be an old underground bomb shelter—a perfect space for a wine cellar and tasting room. My client filled it with over 2,000 bottles of world-class wine. At the conclusion of a seven-day photo shoot, the support staff was invited to enjoy a glass of wine in the cellar.

THE THEATER

A movie theater already existed in the original house, where, reportedly, Soviet officials sat around watching old 1950s movies. We discovered the movie equipment concealed behind a wall. The viewing room was cramped and spartan, so we decided to build a state-of-the-art theater in the new addition to the house.

I imported the top home theater designer in the United States, Theo Kalomirakis, to create a new, private palace of entertainment. The elaborate detailing and rich decorative materials reflect the décor of late 19th- and early 20th-century theaters, but the technology is strictly state of the art. When visitors walk into the theater, a double curtain opens like in an old movie house, the 20th Century Fox studio fanfare plays, and a special lighting sequence begins. It's quite fabulous, and all controlled by a computer.

But, talk about a headache. We hired a Ukrainian electrical engineer away from his underpaid position as a professor of engineering. (People over there are over-educated for the kinds of jobs they're able to find.) He was to function as the full-time maintenance man over all the technology on the property.

I soon discovered that whenever I sent anything that was electrical or in any way technological, the first thing the engineer did was take it apart to see how it worked. For instance, I once returned to Kiev to discover he'd completely taken apart a DVD player I'd sent and was trying to put it back together.

Because the technology for the theater was going to be very expensive, I wanted a top-quality expert to install it. I don't know anything about electronics or technology,

I collaborated with theater designer Theo Kalomirakis on the exquisite design of the home theater. The drama and fantasy created in the elaborate theater are the product of Theo's perfect sense of proportion, resulting in a space that looks and feels large and grand.

69

but I wanted a turnkey job so it would be easy for the owner to operate. I called a source I trusted in Los Angeles and said, "If Steven Spielberg needed to have a theater set up, who would he use?" I hired the man my source recommended, Robert Eitel.

The expert came to Kiev and worked on a computer—just type, type, type for days. It nearly drove me crazy. I didn't think anything could be that complicated. There are about 15 different light settings in the theater with a light behind every little piece of molding.

Every aspect of the installation required so much time. Getting the electric curtains to open on cue took days. One would open in one direction and one in the other direction, or the back one would open before the front one. It was all about getting everything programmed just right in the computer. I would think, this guy's going to fly back to California, and what if something goes wrong?

opposite: Under the ornate dome and the glittering chandelier, guests sink into plush seating. Selected Scalamandré fabrics and the owner's discreetly incorporated monogram embellish the walls. *left*: In the lobby, George Hurrell portraits of actors Jean Harlow and Clark Gable evoke the mood of glamorous 1930s Hollywood.

During all this work on the system, the Ukrainian engineer was supposed to have been following every detail, keeping track of everything. We thought we were finished, and the technology expert returned to California.

A few days later, I was on the second floor and I heard a weird sound—like "ruummm-BUM!"—then all the lights went out. I ran downstairs through the dark house, and out of the basement emerged the engineer. His hair was frizzed and singed all around the edges. I thought he had been electrocuted. He couldn't explain what happened because he only spoke Russian, and I don't.

He had blown out all the technology, all the equipment, the endless hours of computer input. He crashed the whole system. So, the technical expert from Los Angeles returned to Kiev, and we started all over with new equipment, new wiring, new programming. It was more than a power surge. It was a power disaster.

A Villa in Acapulco

BEAUTY BY THE BAY

Dian and I prepare to board the doctor's private jet, destination Acapulco. This was a great time for us and for our business. The possibilities seemed endless.

ACAPULCO opened my eyes to a whole new world of privilege and indulgence — a world that can suck you in and redirect your outlook on life. In the early 1980s, my former wife and design partner, Dian, and I had taken a giant career step forward by creating two model apartments for The Houstonian, then the newest luxury high-rise condominium in Houston. One of the stylish units we designed was purchased, intact, by an affluent Chicago doctor seeking a pied-à-terre in Houston while his wife was undergoing treatment at the Texas Medical Center.

We were flattered when the doctor described the apartment as "a work of art," and asked me to "do some work" on his house in Acapulco. Due to the low-key way he expressed it, I thought he needed a bedspread or something. Still, it sounded like fun, so Dian and I joined the doctor and his wife on their private plane for a weekend trip to Acapulco, the glamorous Mexican city on the Pacific Ocean.

The doctor's house was perched on the side of a hill in the upper, older part of Las Brisas, a famous resort known for pink jeeps, private swimming pools for the guests, and fantastic views of Acapulco Bay. However, as villas go, the doctor's was not particularly memorable. It had six basic, hotel-like bedrooms, three directly above the other three, and a living-dining room space positioned above an open patio-like area. It reminded me of a 1950s motel. I started to wonder what he would want us to do.

One evening as the sun was setting, the doctor and I were standing at the edge of their property drinking margaritas and looking out at Acapulco Bay. The lights twinkled below us, and a giant cruise ship was slowly pulling into the port. I was thinking, "Man, oh man, is this the life!"

"I've been everywhere," the doctor said, "and I believe this bay has the most beautiful view in all the world." I agreed wholeheartedly.

Then he turned and looked back at the house and said something incredible: "I want you to make this house equal to the view."

I didn't know exactly what that meant, but it certainly sounded like a marvelous opportunity, definitely a lot better than buying a couple of new bedspreads. When I asked him for

right: The view of Acapulco Bay is so magnificent, you almost didn't notice how uninspired and conventional the villa appeared. The original house was boxy and boring.

below: The owner of the villa requested that I create a home that would be equal in beauty to his awesome view of Acapulco Bay. Inspired by this vision, I transformed the house by softening the boxy edges and allowing the architecture to flow. Local craftsmen added marvelous details.

above: This house, like many in Mexico, had hundreds of steps taking you to the five different levels throughout the property.

opposite: By taking the original, merely functional steps and turning them into a grand staircase, I changed an unattractive necessity into a feature that made the entire house majestic and beautiful.

details, his answer was an interior designer's dream-come-true:

"Just let your imagination run wild," he said. "There's no limit in time or budget."

I couldn't believe it, but I attacked this challenge in the same way I would later tackle all my other big projects. I tried to blend the personality of the clients and the character of the location, and then apply these aspects to the space or house I was designing. This couple had owned their Acapulco house for 20 years; they had a history there. However, their house was plain and functional. I wanted to turn it into a gracious villa, and give it a sense of heritage.

The transformation took more than two years. We added a wing, towers, several staircases, including a grand staircase at the side of the house, arches framing the spectacular views of the bay, and a beautiful pool. Eventually, vines would cover the walls, the gardens would fill in, and the house would look as if it had been there for a very long time.

This period marked the beginning of a change in my personal life. I had to spend weeks at a time in Acapulco while Dian preferred to remain in Houston. This would become a pattern for our personal and professional relationship, and, sadly, we divorced in 1987 after 16 years and two great children.

I felt strongly that I wanted the villa to honor the culture and artistry of Mexico, and to be reflective of its beautiful name: Casa en la Sombre de la Cruz, which means "house in the shadow of the cross." Toward that end, I went all over Mexico looking for silversmiths, potters, and other artisans whose work we could translate into the design of the house. I was particularly interested in stonework.

Filled with anticipation, I visited several stone quarries. I had read about Michelangelo going to a marble quarry and being able to look at the ground and select just the right piece of stone. Needless to say, although I waited patiently for divine inspiration, it just looked like dirt to me.

Getting to quarries and transporting the stones back to the house posed problems. Once I rode with a man in a pickup truck out in the middle of nowhere, in the depths of Mexico. As we drove across a field with huge rocks, bumping all the way, I thought, "This is a bad idea—where are we going?" I could not see any sign of a quarry. My driver spoke only a little bit of English, and I spoke no Spanish, so I couldn't ask.

When we finally reached the quarry, I expected to see equipment and lots of workers. Instead, I found two men who apparently had arrived on bicycles via the same bumpy route

above: The pool is an important feature of every villa in Acapulco and, ideally, it should be simple and practical, yet grand. I believe this pool achieves that. It's big enough for swimming laps, yet its unique shape echoing the "cut out" designs on the front of the house makes it a glistening work of art.

right: A gold cross emblem adorns the bottom of the pool (representing the name of the villa: Casa en la Sombre de la Cruz), adding a bit of color and design to the classic aquamarine tiles.

opposite: The hand-carved door frame surrounds a beautiful two-story door, providing entry to the library.

right: Hand carved stone railings added to the balconies gave the house a sort of modern-yet-antique Spanish Colonial feeling.
below: I kept the lovely open-to-the-garden aspect of the house, but "framed" the porches with carved stone, shaped in simple designs. The landscaping and tropical blooms softened the look of the stone. The local stone carvers work in the same manner and with the same tools as they have for generations.
opposite: We created stone-clad arches that perfectly frame the close-up views of the gardens and patio with the stunning vista of Acapulco Bay in the distance.

we had taken. They were shaving rock off the edge of a hill with a long tool. They would hammer a series of holes into the rock until part of it fell off. And that's how we got all the stone for the house. They trucked it in, and most of the stone carving was done on the job site.

The large truck used to transport the stone couldn't make it up the roads that wind to the top of the hill in Las Brisas where my client's house was located. So, they had to off-load the stone onto a smaller pickup truck. Finally, to reach the house from the road, the workers had to walk down the equivalent of three flights of steps, carrying the stones on their backs or by hand. All the concrete needed for the project was carried in five-gallon buckets.

The whole process, from quarrying to carving and laying the stone, went on for months. I think this must have been a little bit like building the pyramids. Still, for a long time, we employed a lot of people to build that house, much longer than we anticipated.

But Acapulco was not all work and no play. There were fascinating people, great parties, and new experiences. I met many of the rich, famous, and infamous through Rocchi, a celebrated Italian sculptor I commissioned to do a sundial in the form of a female figure named "La Meridiana." Rocchi, who split his time between Acapulco and Portofino, Italy, brought patrons together at lavish lunches he served under a big thatched roof, or *palapa*, near his pool and boccie ball court.

Rocchi lived in a charming, rustic house he built in a modest, working-class part of Acapulco. When people he knew arrived in Acapulco, they'd call him and say they wanted to see him during the visit. I know because I did this, too. He would invariably say, "Can you come for lunch today?" So you would go and spend the most delightful four hours having lunch at Rocchi's place with a hodgepodge of interesting guests. I met everybody there. And the food was fabulous, pure Italian, like nothing you ever get in Mexico.

Rocchi made terrific margaritas that had a secret ingredient. When we were having cocktails before lunch or dinner, we would go into his studio to see what he was working on. It was

always something interesting, like a sculpture of the president of some South American country. Basically, although Rocchi hardly spoke a word, he was selling his art the whole time you were there. But it didn't matter. We all enjoyed the camaraderie.

One of the "firsts" I experienced in Acapulco was a massage. I was a bit nervous about it, so I chose my underwear carefully and hoped I would get to keep it on. Later, when a friend asked me how I liked the massage, I said, "Well, the last time anybody did that to me, I married her."

And then, there were the sunsets. That glorious sunset in Acapulco happened every day and was treated as a reason to celebrate. There was always someone to entertain, or to entertain you, with margaritas. After Acapulco, I quit drinking.

5 A Newport Schoolhouse

SAVED FROM THE WRECKER'S BALL

TACKLING a historic restoration wasn't on my radar screen the day in the early 1990s when I decided to check out a project one of my clients, a real estate developer, was starting in Newport, Rhode Island, without me. He had told me about it, but said the budget was just too small to include my services.

The Clarke School was one of those classic, red brick, early 20th-century public schoolhouses reminiscent of those many of us attended. (It also looks like the libraries Andrew Carnegie built all over the United States at about the same time.) It is located about three blocks from the Newport waterfront where hundreds of luxurious yachts and graceful sailboats dock in the summer. The steep, monumental steps lead to a heavy front door in the center of the building, and immense double-hung windows are balanced on either side. You can almost imagine those windows, open in early June, catching the ocean breezes, and kids daydreaming and yearning to get out of school for the summer.

But the school had outlived its usefulness, and was about to be rehabilitated in an ordinary, keep-the-cost-down way. It had already been used briefly as an office building, undergoing some haphazard renovations. Now it was going to be reincarnated as affordable housing for senior citizens.

I had done development projects with this client all over the country, but this one, he told me, really didn't warrant a designer. He said the budget was really tight and the project was going to be pretty vanilla and plain.

It was one of those deals where the numbers just didn't work because it wasn't big enough to hold many apartments. Another problem was the school's designation as a historical building. The tug between development and preserving history plays itself out over and over. We live in an economics-based society and, if the economics don't work, who's going to pay to maintain a building that no longer has any use? This was high-yield real estate in a wonderful resort community.

Because of its historic designation, the exterior of the building could not be changed or expanded to increase the number of apartments. However, the interior was pretty much up for grabs. A mammoth 12-foot-wide hallway with gothic-style arches and beautiful old hardwood

The building had a 12-foot-wide center hallway with large spaces on each side that had once been classrooms. Preserving the floorboards, the arches, and the cabinetry, we moved the walls in to provide space for kitchens and baths in the classrooms-turned-apartments. The tops of the walls were slanted back toward the original ceiling. The slanted extensions were then finished to look like old-fashioned school lockers.

floors ran through the center of the building. Large spaces that had formerly been classrooms opened off the hallway.

When I arrived, my client's workmen had just begun demolishing the interior. I called my client on my cell phone as I watched them tearing the place apart.

"This is breaking my heart," I said to him. "This building still has all the original slate blackboards and batten-bead wainscoting. They are ripping out these huge cabinets with glass doors that people are paying a fortune to reproduce!"

"What do you want me to do?" my client asked.

"Hire me to coordinate this project," I said, "… and I don't care if I ever get paid. I want to reclaim these interiors, and reuse every possible material in some way."

In a predictable, bottom-line response, the developer gave me the old line that saving and reusing materials would be more expensive. I responded with "No, it's not. I want to save the bookcases and the blackboards."

Why in the world would anyone want to save slate blackboards, the developer asked. I didn't have an answer at that moment, but I knew I could do something with those huge slabs of slate. Finally, even though I had never been involved with a historic preservation project, I convinced him to let me try, and the Clarke School got a new lease on life.

In order to add a bathroom and kitchen in each classroom-turned-apartment, a few feet had to be taken from each side of the central hall. We wanted to preserve the hall's wide, open feeling, so instead of extending the new walls all the way to the ceiling, we built them up only part of the way and then slanted them back to the original wall. We finished the hall sides to look like old-fashioned school lockers.

My creativity went into high gear studying the blackboards that still hung on the classroom walls. Also, running along the bottom of the blackboards were these beautifully detailed oak chalk trays. With the help of Paul Beaulieu and Michael Abbott, we decided to create the signage for the entire building with these blackboards. To the side of the door to each apartment, we hung a small blackboard with the unit number on it and chalk in the chalk tray for leaving messages, like "I've gone to lunch" or "Sorry you weren't here when I stopped by."

Historic preservation restrictions weren't the only design guidelines that had to be observed. There are many regulations to follow when designing for senior housing, including those specified in the Americans with Disabilities Act. To be ADA-compliant, the building had to have a ground-level entrance.

The developer renovated the basement to create an entryway and other new spaces. For flooring, we cut up and laid more of the old slate blackboards, and the recycled batten-bead wainscoting added character to the walls. Frankly, I've never seen a basement look so good!

Some of the glass-door oak cabinets we salvaged were installed in what was to be the community room to store games and projects. We moved other cabinets into the central hallway and then placed an ad in the Newport newspaper asking local residents to bring us any Clarke School memorabilia that they might have saved. Many people responded with wonderful things that we displayed in the hall cabinets, creating a little museum about the school.

As details about the restoration filtered out, the Clarke School project became a popular topic around town. When the marketing campaign for the senior housing facility began, the apartments filled quickly. I was very proud of this project, because not only did we create affordable housing for seniors that is both charming and luxurious, we preserved the spirit of the Clarke School.

Since then, my client, the developer, has done several more historic restorations around New England, adapting existing buildings into affordable senior housing. But I've never had to convince him again to include me. I've been on board for every one from the outset.

The red brick Clarke School in Newport, Rhode Island, was built in a style popular for schools and libraries in the early 1900s. Built around 1906, it was turned into affordable housing for seniors in 1995.

6 London Surprises

THE OLD AND THE NEW

Oh, to be in England now that April's there
And whoever shops in England sees grand antiques everywhere.
(with apologies to Robert Browning)

above: Afternoon tea at Brown's Hotel is always part of a trip to London for Chad and Courney Stubbs. *opposite, clockwise, from top left:* Courtney, dressed in an antique christening gown, is the most precious thing in a vignette in my former antiques shop, Ancient Age Antiques (circa 1982); Bettie Jo Stubbs, left, joins her grandchildren, Chad and Courtney, and me for a family tradition—taking time out from hectic shopping for antiques and art in London to enjoy tea at Brown's; Marion Sword and I take a break from shopping for an "elegant" lunch along Portobello Road; My son Chad and I join the throngs hunting for antiques along Portobello Road in the mid–1980s.

APRIL, August, even January—I love to be in England and apologize to no one for my affinity for all things English.

I'm a complete Anglophile. London is the place I am most comfortable. It's the people, the signs, everything. It's my heritage. Every time I get on a bus, I feel like I'm looking at my cousins. Anything that requires me to be in London is a gift. Even now when I'm going to Moscow and can select any bridge city—Paris, Amsterdam—I find the trip is bearable if I can have an overnight in London, even just for 24 hours. It's my place to recharge.

My love affair with England began in 1981 in a dilapidated warehouse crammed with antiques in Bellaire, Texas, a proud town surrounded years ago by the sprawling city of Houston. I was visiting with antiques dealer Marion Sword, who made four buying trips to England a year and had designers standing in line when she unloaded a container. I told her that her business sounded like such fun that "if you ever decide to retire, call me."

By the time I returned to my office, Marion had called. She did want to sell the company and offered to work with me for a year to teach me the business.

When I said, "Call me," I was thinking this might happen in the future. I was 30 years old, married with an 8-year-old and a baby, and had a pretty big design business. But, it was an opportunity I couldn't refuse.

Our first "session" was a buying trip to London. I remember thinking since I was half Marion's age, I could work twice as fast on trips. So on my first British shopping experience with her, I thought we'd take a night flight, land the next morning, and then take the rest of the day off to rest and regroup. But, no, she hit the ground running. We went straight to the train station, where we caught a train north to Leeds, then all the way up to York, buying antiques all along the way. Soon I learned that we could pass on something in York on Monday, and by Saturday we'd see it at London's popular Portobello Market at twice the price.

top, right: My daughter Courtney and I found what must have been the last Christmas tree in London during a 1999 holiday visit. *above*: Chad and Courtney decorated the tree in the London flat my client loaned to us for the Christmas holidays.

The days all began at seven in the morning. Shopkeepers would open early for us because Marion had booked ahead. Similarly, other sellers would meet us at seven in the evening and give us dinner (sandwiches, in their shop), while we were buying, until about 11 o'clock. We would go to the fairs where we'd start at 6 AM with a flashlight. We were buying all these beautiful things and hauling a lot of them around, but she could work twice as fast and keep going twice as long as I could.

Greater insight into Marion's methods came the first time I visited London's famed Portobello Road Market with her. We were buying everything in sight—silver-top bottles, silver boxes, inlaid boxes—as fast as we could go, just trying to get in front of the next buyer.

After several hours, I said, "Could we go to lunch?"

"Oh, O.K.," she said. "We can stop now."

It was a cold day, but she walked into the street and announced, "I brought lunch." She pulled a ham sandwich from each pocket of her old wool coat with a Peter Pan collar and one big button at the top. Together, we sat on some steps and ate, then back to work we went. Ten minutes, max, for lunch.

Whether you're a collector or an antiques dealer, the hunt is a great part of the fun. The buying was hard work, but I've never had that much fun. You would discover some of the most unusual things, like the two wooden pigs—they looked like flying pigs—that originally had been a butcher's sign. They faced each other and had big bows, one blue and one pink. I sold those babies like nobody's business.

GOOD NEWS/BAD NEWS

The fun that started in 1981—the antiques business—came to a screeching halt around 1986, when Houston's high-flying economy hit the skids. There were no more designers standing in line to check out my cache, no buyers knocking on my door.

But there's an old saying that when one door closes, another door opens. Sometimes it just takes a while. That door opened wide in 1994 when my former client, the Ukrainian oil trader, whose penthouse I designed in the early 1980s, bought the dacha in his homeland. Then, in

1999, a few years after we completed the dacha project, my hopes soared when he bought an apartment in London. That was the good news.

The bad news was it was already fully furnished, right down to the sheets and towels. The flat was one of the redevelopment projects of brothers Charles and Jeremy Tyler, of Tyler London Ltd. They purchase older flats, remodel the apartments into meticulously built-out, contemporary homes, then decorate the interiors in a simple, yet opulent, clean-lined style.

I was especially disappointed since there was nothing I would have enjoyed more than a design project in London, but I also knew my client. Of course, as I half suspected, the second day after he purchased the apartment, he called to tell me it needed to be personalized for him. "This is too stark, too simple," he said. "Come help me.'"

So I flew to London, and went shopping at Harrods, Hèrmes, and Gucci. I bought the best in contemporary design—new china, sterling flatware, crystal, even a Bosendorfer baby grand piano from Harrods. I did everything I could, short of completely redecorating, to give the apartment more of the feeling of luxury and warmth he wanted.

For the next three years, my client generously let me stay in his apartment whenever I was in London. I think I slept there more than he did.

A sensuous, contemporary tone was established in the entry of this London apartment with the seamless appearance of creamy-colored, book-matched marble floors.

My son Chad, daughter Courtney, and I spent a magical Christmas in London, arriving at the apartment on Christmas Eve. Courtney and I went out into the night and found what must have been the last Christmas tree in the city. We decorated it with whatever we could find at the grocery store. Then we walked down Knightsbridge Road to attend Christmas church services.

That holiday trip was in 1999 when we were all anticipating the arrival of the new millennium. London was really charged up. They had the Millennium Dome, and there was the big fear of Y2K. People were afraid to fly on January 1, 2000, but that's the day we flew home. Nothing ever scares me. I guess that's why I've had all these adventures.

One of my least favorite adventures came on another trip to England, this time with Courtney and my sister, Sugar. We went to the south of England to a place called New Forest, even though it was settled in the year 1400. We were staying at a friend's charming cottage in the forest, and since we were in the country, we thought we should try English riding. We called the stable to book a lesson, and they asked for our weights.

Upon arrival, we were given the proper little hats and crops, and they brought out handsome horses for Courtney and Sugar. Then they brought out old Shamus, the horse they deemed appropriate for me. That was really his name. He was tall, with big, hairy feet and looked like a Clydesdale. I was practically doing the splits getting on because he was so wide. We rode into the forest, and the instructor said, "Shall we trot?" I thought, "No, don't trot!" I was bouncing from one side of that horse to the other. Sugar and Courtney did very well and loved the outing, but I had a miserable experience. Then and there, I decided I'd stick to designing.

A LONDON DREAM-COME-TRUE

Predictably, my longtime client eventually decided to gut his London flat and start over. He wanted it to be the most luxurious place you'd ever stepped into—as opulent as the mansion in Kiev, but contemporary, not traditional.

Contemporary. In England. If ever I faced a design challenge, this was it.

First of all, contemporary is really not my style. If there is a style I'm most comfortable with, it's English county. So much of what I love about England is the history and that patina of age. I think my vision of doing a project in London was designing a cozy library or a chintz-filled bedroom, so I was really being stretched.

Courtesy Tyler London Ltd.

Courtesy Tyler London Ltd.

opposite: With the help of the development firm, Tyler London, I was able to pull off an impeccable contemporary redesign of an apartment in one of the most traditional cities in the world.
left: In the master bedroom, I combined subtle and restrained colors, textures, and finishes to create a retreat of total comfort and luxury.
above: A glossy black Bosendorfer baby grand piano is the solitary classical element in the contemporary London residence.

left: For an accent of color in the mostly neutral living room, and a touch of nature's beauty, I stacked fresh green apples into a mound in a wide bowl on the minimalist cocktail table. *above*: Fiber optic lighting in the ceiling of the dining room perfectly illuminates each place setting on the table with carefully positioned, tiny beams of light. A glass wall divides the dining room from the ultra-modern kitchen that almost looks like a sculpture.

right: The fireplace seems to float in the center of the apartment, adding a sense of spark and warmth to contrast with the cool, sleek finishes of the interiors.

opposite, bottom left and right: Efficiency is not sacrificed for style in the Bulthaup kitchen. A Bang & Olufsen television and sound system, Krups espresso machine, and American walnut flooring complete the space. Preparing a meal in this kitchen is like cooking inside a work of art.

opposite, top: The precision-crafted stainless steel wine closet is back-lit to make it an eye-catching element in the striking kitchen design.

The challenge proved exhilarating; the possibilities, amazing. Rather than the familiar antiques shops and traditional resources, I had to look elsewhere for purely contemporary design. I selected finishes and furnishings, and the Tyler brothers implemented the plans with speed and perfection. Sometimes it was like a trip into the unknown for this designer from Texas. Contemporary design looks so simple, so easy, but creating those illusions can be quite difficult.

I'd toss out something like, "Wouldn't it be nice if the grain in the marble continued all the way down the hall floor?" and Charles Tyler would say, "Well, we'll just book-match it. We'll buy an entire block of marble in France, have it custom cut and lay the tiles so they match up perfectly." The finished floor looked like something that was drawn instead of separate slabs. The problem was if you broke one of those squares — for example, if you moved a piano across the floor and cracked one of them — the whole floor would be ruined. You would have to get a whole new block of marble, and start over.

On this project, perfection became the ultimate goal. There was no tolerance for error in anything. For example, a certain wall finish took about 17 steps to achieve the desired look, and then the last step was the application of automobile wax, which was then hand-buffed. The final surface felt cold to the touch — like marble. Once, the Tylers didn't like the way the paint looked after it had been rolled on a ceiling, so they had it repainted with a brush, the stroke always going in the same direction for a flawless effect.

Despite all the sleek, hard surfaces, I still had to make the place feel cozy and inviting. So I layered textures, starting with a rich wool fabric covering some walls and tightly woven, commercial-looking carpet topped with area rugs, and a fur throw under the piano. All these things remained true to the contemporary ethic, even the two layers of draperies at the windows.

When you come in the front door of the apartment, there's that kind of "thud" you hear when you slam the door to a Bentley — that sense of solid elegance. It was quite an adventure, being that kind of a purist.

Still, my interpretation of contemporary was anything but cold. It was actually quite lavish, with very tactile fabrics, all soft and comfortable. I covered an entire wall in the master bedroom in a man-made suede, like Ultrasuede, which seemed to give a soft, but solid, feeling to the whole room.

The biggest thrill in the design, however, was the lighting and the technology behind it: cold cathode and fiber optics. All the ceilings "floated," meaning they were suspended without touching the walls, and the cold cathode lighting was tucked in behind the ceiling, giving the

Courtesy Tyler London Ltd.

Courtesy Tyler London Ltd.

Courtesy Tyler London Ltd.

feeling of being either in a space ship or on a fabulous yacht. Cathode is a lot like neon with a continuous light stream in a tube, but it can be dimmed and neon cannot.

Working with fiber optics specialists Absolute Action, I was excited about the results. One of the real challenges for a designer is to place lighting over a dining room table. First, you position the light fixture, then the table comes in, and invariably you want it to go to the left or right. But you have to place it under the chandelier that's already hanging there.

But, with fiber optics, we could place the dining table wherever we wanted it, and completely set it with dishes and flatware. The fiber optic lighting cables had already been laid out in the ceiling, and the Absolute Action team came in with a drill and a little hand-held vacuum cleaner. I'd say, "Put a light over this plate," and they would drill a little pinhole while the vacuum sucked up all the dust, reach into the ceiling with a tool to pull a fiber optic cable into the hole, put a cover on it and point a stream of light down just the size of the plate. We could light each plate, the centerpiece—whatever I pointed out.

They lit the piano keyboard with three lights, and spotlighted the artwork. In a photograph of the room, the lights in the ceiling show up, but when you're in the space, you don't notice the light source. You're not even sure where the light is coming from. It's great. The whole living room was lit from one 250-watt bulb that's in a closet, and the cables went out from there.

The system's flexibility allowed me to do floor lighting that grazed over sheer panels woven with metallic threads. We washed over the gold threads with gold light. It was so dramatic; it was almost sensory overload.

The magic continued in the kitchen. For the most part, it remained the same as it had been originally redesigned, but the wine closet was turned into a work of art. The kitchen was in full view of the dining room and the kitchen lighting was too bright, almost glary. To add visual warmth to the high-tech space, I placed a theatrical gel over the lights inside the wine cabinet, giving the bottles and stainless steel racks a warm golden glow visible through the glass door.

When the apartment was finished, I wanted to have it photographed. I knew exactly what I needed—minimal floral arrangements in simple, elegant vases. No over-accessorizing, just six calla lilies in a perfect Baccarat vase to set the right tone. For a touch of color in the mainly neutral setting, I bought six bags of green apples in Harrods Food Hall. I prefer that the owner not be around when the photographs are being taken, but this time my client was there.

I started arranging the apples in a big, gorgeous bowl on the cocktail table, and my client said, "Nobody puts green apples in the living room. That's going to look stupid."

I explained that they were only to add a little color for the photos, but he continued to protest, saying he didn't want them on his table. I told him to please go away while we were photographing. He retreated but kept coming back, first asking how many apples were in the bowl, then if he should buy artificial or real apples. I reminded him that he didn't like green apples but added that fresh ones would last about four weeks.

After the photography session, I dumped the apples in the trash. When my client saw they were gone, he ordered me to put them back in the bowl, insisting he never said he didn't like green apples. When you buy apples at Harrods, it's worth going back into the trash to get them—which I did. Also, from then on, every time I arrived at the apartment, the bowl on the cocktail table was filled with green apples.

opposite: The guest bedroom is reminiscent of a perfectly appointed stateroom on a magnificent yacht.
above: Book-matched French marble in the guest bath brings a feeling of unity to the private space. Carefully selected natural materials add a sense of Eastern tranquility.

THE LADY & THE TEXAN

I have made many friends in London, but none more intriguing than interior designer and author Lady Henrietta Spencer-Churchill, daughter of the 11th Duke of Marlborough. We met at the Chelsea Design Center at a board meeting for the International Interior Design Association.

I arrived late for a wine-and-cheese reception in the Brunschwig & Fils showroom. I didn't see anyone I knew, so I stood in a corner, wishing I had skipped this event. Then, this very attractive woman came over and said, in her perfect British accent, "I don't really enjoy affairs like this."

And I said, "You and me, both!" She responded with something like, "I guess it is something we must do."

So while this woman and I began chatting, James Steinmeyer, an interior designer from Beaumont, Texas, came up and said, "Bill, have you met Lady Henrietta Spencer-Churchill?"

"No, I haven't," I answered, and looked out into the crowd, expecting to see some gray-haired lady wearing a mink stole.

"This is Lady Henrietta Spencer-Churchill," James said, gesturing toward the young woman I had been visiting with. I immediately choked up, then sputtered, "Oh, gosh, I'm sorry. I didn't introduce myself."

Later I learned that the British do not consider it appropriate to walk up to a stranger at a party and introduce yourself; instead you wait to be introduced. So I had inadvertently done the proper thing. She said, "Hello, I'm Henrietta," and put out her hand, which I took and said, "Hi, I'm Bill Stubbs." I blurted out something about hoping to see her during the conference, and she said, "Why don't we have lunch tomorrow?"

So we met for a lunch that lasted two and a half hours. It was delightful, but I still wasn't quite sure what we had in common. The conference the next day was to take place at one of England's most spectacular estates, Blenheim Palace, which happened to be Lady Henrietta's ancestral home.

During lunch, she asked me to come a little early, before the other participants would arrive for the meeting. I was flattered beyond belief—first, that someone of Henrietta's stature and appeal would even want to talk to me, and second, I was going to see her at Blenheim, my favorite stately house in the world. From the first time I ever toured Blenheim—before I ever knew Henrietta—I loved everything about it. Why, they commissioned Thomas Chippendale to make their cabinets. It's like the origin of my favorite style of furnishings.

The next day, my host for the visit loaned me her Mercedes-Benz to drive to Blenheim. When I drove up to the humongous gate and gatehouse, I wondered if I should buy a ticket. I rolled down the window, not sure what to say, and, to my amazement, the guard said, "Mr. Stubbs? Lady Henrietta is expecting you."

I followed his directions, driving past the coach stop, through two more gates, past the cows, and finally winding up on the crunchy gravel drive at the front door to the palace.

As I pulled up, Henrietta stepped out to greet me. I felt so special, but I still didn't know why she wanted me there. Soon, all the IIDA members began arriving in motor coaches, and Henrietta and I were standing there greeting them. I kept thinking I should be sitting at a desk writing out name tags.

The conference center at Blenheim is in the old stables, complete with a tea room that prepares the meals. (Even the bottled water has a Blenheim label.) When it was time for lunch, Henrietta said: "Bill, we're a little short-staffed today," and I thought, this is it, she wants me to work in the kitchen. But then she said, "Why don't you and I help serve lunch?"

Well, it didn't take long for the whispering to start—we had met at the reception, had lunch the next day, greeted the guests together at the entrance, and now we were serving lunch. Later when the picture-taking started, she asked me to stand next to her for a photograph. Finally, I just accepted that she enjoyed my company as much as I enjoyed hers.

Henrietta and I became really good friends. She has come to Houston on several occasions, and we have been together a number of times in London. Once when my daughter, sister, and I were there, Henrietta asked us to dinner at her townhouse in Chelsea. She barbecued chicken on the grill outside—there wasn't any help—and we ate in the kitchen. It was just like going over to any friend's house for dinner—really nice and easy.

One time Henrietta invited me for a weekend in the country. I didn't know what that meant, so I didn't go. I would not have known what to wear or what to do. I figured a weekend at Blenheim would require a whole new wardrobe. And you might have to know how to ride a horse or shoot a gun—which someone from Texas should know. But I don't.

Part of the delight I find in my frequent trips to London is the friendship I've enjoyed with Lady Henrietta Spencer-Churchill, who is also an interior designer.

7 Kona, Hawaii

NO REST IN PARADISE

opposite: The tranquility of Hawaii's ocean view slowly soothed my hyper and harried countenance after the long flight from Houston.

THE TROPICAL Garden of Eden called Hawaii may be paradise to those who fall under its romantic spell, but it's not my idea of heaven-on-earth. For starters, I'm just not a beachy, laid-back kind of person. When I travel, I want places to see and things to do; I like to keep moving.

Also, part of my disenchantment with Hawaii harks back to my first trip there in the late 1980s, the first two-week vacation my wife Dian and I had ever planned after 10 years of marriage. We went with another couple and arrived at the beautiful resort hotel, the Hana Maui, during a torrential rainstorm. Then we had to walk to our bungalows lugging our baggage, in the rain. Suddenly Hawaii didn't seem very charming, and it only got worse.

Because of the time change, I woke up at five the next morning, but I wasn't able to just kick back, relax and watch the sun rise. Instead, I woke up my buddy Jim, the other husband in our foursome, and we decided to go for a hike. During our trek, I slipped and fell down the side of a lava cliff for probably 50 feet, the equivalent of a five-story building, grabbing frantically as I went down, but unable to catch hold of anything. All the skin on the front of my body was scraped; I was just one big open wound. For the rest of the trip, I was in agony. I couldn't even pick up our luggage, since all the skin on my hands was gone, too.

So, Hawaii has never been one of my favorite places.

Little did I know when I went to Fort Worth, Texas, to meet with potential clients that I would soon be spending a lot of time back in Hawaii. At first, they talked about possibly remodeling either their primary residence, a comfortable, 1970s ranch-style house in Fort Worth, or the almost-new contemporary house next door which they had bought. Then, he mentioned his dream of building an enormous, Polynesian-style house on their ranch land outside Fort Worth.

I had just met this couple and we were already talking about two very different houses and a possible Texas ranch house that would look like it's in Hawaii. While I was trying to sort this out, one of them said, "We wish you could see our boat. We really like the way it's designed and decorated." That seemed like an important piece to this puzzle.

Their yacht was docked in Fort Lauderdale, Florida, so the next time I had to go to Miami

on business, I detoured by Fort Lauderdale to check it out. They were right; it was fabulous, with a main salon, dining room, eat-in gourmet kitchen, media room, three staterooms, and three crew rooms for the full-time captain and crew. Everything was well designed in a warm, contemporary style, rich with teak and brass. I was beginning to get a handle on their tastes.

At our next meeting in Fort Worth, the couple told me they had decided that for our first job together, they wanted me to redecorate the villa they had just purchased at the Hualalai Four Seasons Resort at Kona on the Big Island of Hawaii. The luxury resort complex included a beautiful beach, a golf course, and a magnificent hotel, as well as the residences. This couple seemed so down-to-earth, it was rather hard for me to picture them leading this globe-trotting lifestyle.

A few weeks later, we met in Hawaii, stayed at the hotel that's part of the resort, and began to plan the redesign of their villa. The tropical style of the residences blends naturally with the lavish garden setting, and each home is positioned to have a splendid view of the ocean, but is shielded from all other houses. You had the illusion that you were isolated on a tropical island, yet at the same time, anything you could wish for was at your beck and call.

I envisioned a sophisticated Hawaiian look for this delightful couple's island home. This sort of tropical design was new for me—it seems like I never get a chance to design the same thing twice, to create a "signature" look for myself, like some designers do. Everything I do is closely related to the place where I'm working or my clients' tastes and personalities—or a combination of both.

For this project, I was inspired by the wife's marvelous sense of style. She had beautiful jewelry with a feeling of antiquity, and she wore a lot of sage and copper colors in all-natural fabrics, like wrinkled linens. During our visits in Fort Worth, I also noticed that she liked some things a little askew and playful—all details that would influence my designs for the Kona house.

One of my primary local sources for textiles and furnishings was Jeanne Marie Imports. The owner, Jeanne Marie, is an attractive antiques dealer who's always fun to be around. She travels to Malaysia and Bali and up into the mountains and buys terrific things, such as huge beds, little copper and bronze beads, beaded handwork, and Balinese ceremonial sarongs woven with gold in geometric patterns.

Never before had any of my clients requested a dark interior, especially in a warm, sunny locale like Hawaii. But this couple loved the dark, rich wall coverings I suggested. The light in Hawaii is very strong, and typically islanders do their interiors in white. That's exactly what the existing color scheme in my client's villa was—white and glary. It makes a place particularly uninteresting at night, sort of like a hospital room with a light on.

Also, in most places located on the ocean, the focus is on the view of the water. Then, at night, the inviting view becomes a big black hole. At the Four Seasons Resort, however, low-level lighting and gas torch lights create a romantic, outdoor setting at night, and I felt I had to honor that quality in the interiors. To achieve this, interior lighting was projected onto the walls and ceiling to look as if it were shining through tree leaves, giving a soft, mottled effect.

opposite: Jeanne Marie, of Jeanne Marie Imports, is my favorite source for unusual, one-of-a-kind decorative pieces in Kona. One can find everything from intricate beadwork to immense carved beds in her shop.

Taking clues from the clients' teak-paneled yacht, I covered and coved every surface, applying a heavy woven grass paper on the ceilings and Brazilian mahogany everywhere for a teak look. Because the wife said she wanted the feeling of sheer curtains blowing in the breeze, I found elegant, gauzy fabrics to hang at the usually open doors and windows and to drape the bed.

To finish the villa, I traveled to Hawaii on a regular basis for a year, and stayed at the Four Seasons Hotel. This sounds like a dream assignment, I'm sure. But when you're alone at a fancy resort hotel, you start to feel a little out of place. Hawaii is a very romantic place, the honeymoon capital of the world, but if you're there by yourself, there's not much to do. That was one of the challenges I faced working in Hawaii. The other was getting things done!

I guess because it's a tropical island, people just operate at a slower speed. Before I arrived, I would set up all these appointments in advance with the wallpaper hanger, the painter, the electrician—and no one would show up. Then, to make matters even more complicated, no one would answer his telephone.

Finally, I would reach the contractor's administrative assistant on the phone and say, "Where is everybody? I faxed and e-mailed the schedule last week."

"Oh, was that today?" she'd say, like it was a big surprise. "I'll try to reach them."

Then, a day later, she would report that the electrician was on the other side of the island for a couple of days and wondered when I was coming back. It was incredibly frustrating, and dealing with this attitude required a lot of discipline for me.

Plus, there was usually just one person to do any particular job—one electrician, one wallpaper hanger. When I told the paper hanger I wanted some silk wall-covering panels cut into squares, rotated a half turn and laid like blocks on the wall, he quit. I had to beg him to come

opposite, top: The deep-toned, textured wallcovering in the spacious living room provides a welcome relief from Hawaii's strong sunlight by day and creates a cozy mood at night.
opposite, lower left: All the room's finishes, even the rice paper screen, seem to whisper of faraway islands and thatched-roof huts.
opposite, lower right: Whimsical figures painted on an exotic, red entertainment armoire make this functional piece of furniture an artistic focal point in the living room.
above: Relaxing on the patio overlooking the water, I was especially pleased that my clients felt an immediate connection with the completed design of their home.

Casual yet sophisticated, the dining room in the house is the "essence of Hawaii" with the tropical breeze catching the gauzy draperies, the lighting throwing leafy patterns on the wall, and, outside, palm trees and the incredible view of the ocean.

Gauzy over-drapes laced with metallic threads can be pulled to the side or stretched out to float over the bed with all the glamour of a vintage Hollywood movie set. Tiny details, such as the capiz shell fringe on the spread, enhance the custom touch.

back, or we were going to have to fly someone in from New York to do it. He tried to explain all the reasons it wouldn't work, but he finally did it, perfectly.

Many of the people who live in Hawaii are transplants who have escaped the stress of urban society. Often, they originally came on a vacation from a cold climate, say Detroit, and wondered, "Why am I living in Detroit when I could live here?" They moved not only to escape the cold, but to live in a permanent vacation land, away from the "rat race." So I guess I always brought a little rat race with me when I arrived to work.

Also, everything is more expensive in Hawaii because most materials come from the mainland. For example, the shutters that look so Polynesian are made in Oregon. In the end, the things I bought in Hawaii were mainly artifacts.

Throughout the process, I showed swatches, fabrics, photocopies of furniture and other materials to the clients for approval, but they never visited while the work was under way. When I do a job, I finish everything to the last detail. In this case, I even selected dishes, flatware, linens, and created a number of different ways to set the table.

Finally, the day came when the clients were coming to see the finished project for the first time. I was so nervous, and, more than ever, worried about pleasing them, since it was my first job for them. They have their own plane, so I had asked them to call me when they were in range.

My compulsive tendencies took over. About an hour before they were due to arrive, I decided all the floors needed one more wipe down. I had sent the maids away and, because the resort supplies cleaning service, there was no mop, vacuum cleaner, or any other cleaning product in the house. So there I was, on my hands and knees with a wash cloth, wiping down the floor, and I realized there was no place where I could reasonably stop. I ended up going over the entire 3,000-square-foot marble floor with a wash cloth.

When you check into the Four Seasons Hotel, they greet you with a tray topped with orchids, two chilled wash cloths for a few refreshing pats, and two little cups of cold nectar. I had decided my clients should have the same presentation, so I had everything ready.

But I was sweating like a pig rubbing down the floor, and I wanted to be all fresh and starched when they arrived. The whole thing was causing me almost to implode; I was so uptight.

Rich ethnic patterns, dark walls, and special architectural elements turned this room, which was considered the least attractive room in the house when we started, into the guest room everyone wants to stay in.

Finally, they called from the plane; still I didn't know at what point they were actually going to appear at the door. I kept going from room to room, moving everything just a little bit, thinking, "How could I have done that?"

I wanted a certain song to be playing when they walked in. We had installed an incredible sound system, so every time the song on the CD would end, I would start playing it again. It was like I was living my life in seven minute increments, through this song. All this time, I just kept racing from room to room, turning the orchids just a bit, adjusting the draperies for the breeze.

At last, I heard them at the garage, and I positioned myself at the top of the stairs, holding the tray of flowers, cool cloths, and nectar.

"Welcome to Haulalai," I said, and handed them their nectar. They walked in the door and stopped. They didn't say a word; they just paused.

My heart stopped. I was thinking: "Why aren't they running from room to room looking at everything?" She was standing in the entrance hall and had taken just two steps.

Finally he said, "This is unbelievable."

"Help!" I thought to myself. "Unbelievable" is not a descriptor. It isn't "I like it" or "I don't like it."

So I said, "In what way?"

"This looks just like us!" he answered.

I just about melted, but then he added, "But I didn't know we looked like this."

What an interesting observation, I thought. I believed he was saying that I had taken every little detail, every essence of what they had transmitted to me, and expressed it all in their home. I thought to myself, "I did it, I did it!"

Then she came in, sat down, and looked around.

"I'm not going to rush this," she said. "I'm going to enjoy each space."

So they just sort of lingered in each room, talking to each other, noticing each detail, and savoring the moment. Finally, she paid me a particularly nice compliment:

"You paid attention to everything I ever said—or didn't say." She later told their friends who had put us together that she had never had a place where she didn't want to move anything because it was perfect.

It took the couple about two hours to go through their three-bedroom villa. They loved everything—the mood lighting, the blowing draperies, the gauzy fabric draped over the bed, the capiz shells sewn like a fringe on the bedspread, every painstaking detail.

Watching them take it all in was such fun. And quite a relief.

opposite: Hawaii can be one of the most relaxing places in the world, but I rarely got to take it easy because I was working. Eventually, I decided I really should steal 15 minutes away from work to go to the beach.

8 An American Trio

TWISTS AND TURNS

EVERY residential project brings new personalities, creative challenges, and twists and turns, whether it's halfway around the world or on the designer's home turf. Three of my made-in-the-USA projects required ditching the expected and reinventing dreams for my clients.

RANCH-STYLE REVISE

When a Houston couple asked me to come out and discuss renovating their house, none of us guessed the discussions would become a friendly Friday night ritual that would continue for more than a year. A lot of ideas were tossed around and a lot of meals shared as a friendship blossomed. It became this thing to look forward to. But we never broke ground, never hammered anything—nothing.

The project seemed to get sidetracked, and suddenly—all in one day—my friends sold the house and bought another one they had always admired. The same day, they called me for help.

It was actually the large, wooded lot they liked—not the house. The house is a rambling ranch-style in a neighborhood where people are tearing down the older one-story houses and many of the trees and building huge mansions.

We walked in and the new owners said, "We do not want to tear this house down," then they added, "but it doesn't work for us at all."

The first problem confronted me the minute I walked through the front door. There was the tiniest vestibule—you could hardly call it an entryway—and it opened into a useless living room. The previous owners' furniture was still there: a little Georgian settee and two Chippendale armchairs arranged by a beautiful fireplace, but the overall effect was one of a most uninviting period parlor, with no room for anything else. There was a small dining room; then came a time-warp 1960s kitchen with turquoise metal cabinets. The house really needed to be reworked, opening up spaces for the family's outgoing lifestyle.

I immediately knew I could rip out the wall between the dining room and kitchen and create the ultimate gathering place, where hosts and guests could all congregate and cook at once. And the space would spill out into the family room.

In a Houston ranch-style redo, the greatest challenge
was creating large-scale comfort in a small living room/entry
space. Two enormous chairs combine with an ample ottoman in
front of the fireplace to make this the owners' favorite spot.

right: Once nondescript, the hall guest bath became an unexpected surprise with an Italian marble mosaic underfoot, unique wall sconces, and a deep, sculpted marble wash bowl. *opposite, clockwise from top left*: Ocher walls, an amber Indian chandelier, and wide hand-planed plank floors give a casual, inviting charm to the dining room in the remodeled Houston home. The star of the kitchen is the striking diamond-patterned floor of random-toned slate, bordered with narrow marble strips, and joined at the corners with hand-fired tiles. Washing dishes becomes a beautiful task in the kitchen's cleanup area with the marble-clad farmhouse sink and overhead Welsh dresser-type china storage. The large kitchen, designed to accommodate multiple cooks and guests, opens to the dining and family rooms on either side —a mellow combination of natural materials and finishes makes it blend handsomely with the other spaces.

But it was the living room that presented the biggest challenge. The husband was convinced it was worthless space. So, my promise to him was — and I wasn't sure how I was going to do this — that I would make that room his favorite place in the house. He believed that was impossible because he wanted space and big things, and he couldn't see how I could do that. But I did!

I decided that the whole space — the vestibule and the little living room — needed to become the entry to the house. You needed to be able to open the front door and be presented with a very grand room. But because of the antique "doll furniture" that was in it, you couldn't imagine anything grand about this room.

I ended up playing visual tricks with the space by using a few oversized pieces in the room. The only furnishings are two huge, comfortable chairs in front of the fireplace with a big, leather ottoman between them. Then, an imposing Chinese armoire and a large country dining table are pushed against one wall. Now the scale of everything is big, and the room seems big and gracious and interesting.

When you walk in, the first thing you see is the dining table with giant candlesticks on it, and, on the wall, a painting the owners love. I added hand-hewn plank floors and a deep terra-cotta color on the walls to set the tone for the entire house — a really nice country kind of opulence.

The owners spend almost every morning in there with their coffee, reading the newspaper in front of a crackling fire when it's cold. It's their favorite room in the house. Just like I promised.

CALIFORNIA DREAMING

A Texas couple searching for a second home in southern California turned to me for some advice. After all, I had already decorated seven other houses for them.

We went "property shopping," looking at lots to build on and houses to buy. We kept coming back to this lovely house in Corona del Mar on a lot we all absolutely loved. It had the most magnificent view of any house I've ever done — what in California is called a "white water view," right on the beach. You could hear the waves crashing; it is like being at Big Sur. But they didn't like the house.

Finally, the couple asked me if the floor plan could be altered to suit them. I really had to think about the house in a different way. I had to see it as a clean slate, not the perfectly good house it actually was.

The first big problem lay just inside the front door: a sunken bar with wrap-around black granite countertops. That was definitely not what the couple wanted for a first impression. But the overriding problem was that their spectacular view could not be seen from the house.

It seemed as if no one noticed the view when the house was originally designed and built. The house had no patio on the side that faced the ocean; in fact, the house had no patio at all. The best view of the ocean was from the kitchen sink — and my client doesn't cook, let alone wash the dishes. The breakfast room, which should ideally overlook the ocean, faced a tacky little concrete courtyard on the opposite side of the house.

I concluded that the whole house needed to be flipped. Because the clients loved everything about the location, from the view to the community, they decided to go for it.

Windows were changed to take in the glorious vista, and a terrace was added for dining al fresco and enjoying the view of the rocky coastline as well as the white water. All the changes, including rearranging the kitchen, produced a sophisticated, seaside residence, a perfect change of pace from the owners' home in Texas.

It's hard to believe that before we remodeled this
California home, there was no terrace, and no way to soak
in this incredible view of the ocean and the coastline.

115

above: A richly colored Persian carpet adds a strong foundation to the otherwise white room, and a period Chinese textile hangs above the fireplace.

right: A monochromatic palette of shades of white brings unity to the living and dining areas in the spacious open living area. Thirty feet of windows flood the space with light and a background of aquamarine water and sky.

opposite: It's hard for me to imagine a home with a more special place than this luxuriously comfortable sitting room, where nature provides the art.

below and right: With a limestone fireplace for cool California nights and woven, swirling-patterned Irish wool sheers draping the iron four-poster bed, the master bedroom also features a sweeping view of the ocean. Lavish bed coverings of caramel Scalamandré fabrics and trim contrast with the delicate antique lace hung at the head of the bed.

opposite, top: I moved this client out of a country house, but I had to bring her saddles along. Downsizing to a Houston high-rise was a little easier because her show saddles now hang like art on the living room wall, ready to take down and ride at rodeo time. The show saddles take center stage on custom-designed brackets with copper fronts detailed with the Texas Lone Star.

opposite, below: Only small touches of the owner's penchant for all things Western show up in the luxurious master bedroom.

URBAN COWGIRL

The saddles are the first clue: The lady loves the rodeo.

They are the first thing a visitor sees — three fancy saddles straddling custom-designed copper-faced brackets mounted on the wall next to a shiny black piano. She might have even tossed her fringed suede chaps over the piano bench when she walked in the door.

But this apartment is not a "back-at-the-ranch, down-home" kind of place. This is a stylish high-rise condo deep in the heart of an upscale Houston neighborhood, quite a change from the 5,500-square-foot suburban home where the owner had lived for 24 years and raised her family. The dark cappuccino-brown walls and overstuffed upholstery in sensuous velvets and tapestries create the interior's luxury and flair, but it's the saddles, Western art, and photographs of family, rodeo friends, and events lining the hallway that provide the flavor.

As a highly successful, on-the-go businesswoman, the owner did not have the time or inclination to handle the move to the city. I took over the transition, from finding the right location for her downsizing move to designing every detail. When I started, her new apartment was a distressed white box. We stripped it to the guts, changed the walls, and reconfigured the space.

The owner loves to cook and entertain, so the kitchen was custom designed to hold her essential utensils and appliances. We measured the counter space she had in her big house and gave her an equivalent amount of workspace in her apartment. Everything was planned to feel instantly familiar, down to the drawer to the left of the sink which holds the same things it did in her house.

One of her wishes was to have a kitchen window, but that proved impossible. However, to compensate, we placed a long granite bar, with an open space above, between the kitchen and the glass-walled living room, so she could look out from the kitchen. Cabinets above the bar house storage on the kitchen side and serve as wine racks and a television shelf on the living room side. Recessed lights illuminate the counter space. From the kitchen, she can see the sky and the treetops, and guests can pull up upholstered bar chairs to visit with the hostess as she cooks.

Downsizing this client from 5,500 to 2,100 square feet was no easy task. Things she no longer needed were eliminated and the rest reorganized, right down to every shoe and every tube of lipstick. One closet is devoted to her wardrobe of elaborate rodeo outfits.

opposite, top: The finishes, materials, and details selected for the kitchen are sophisticated and a little rustic.

opposite, below: Because the condo owner loves to cook, the kitchen was gutted and designed to give her maximum working space and storage. She has as much counter space as she had previously in her large home.

left: Storage above the granite bar houses wine racks and a television set from the living room side. From the kitchen side, the "window" provides a view of the sky and treetops.

below: A gently "aged" hand-rubbed barn wood finish on the kitchen cabinets and subtly rugged hardware reflect the owner's Western taste in a low-key style.

About the drastic paring down, she commented: "My daddy always said you have to let things age before you can throw them out." She admitted she couldn't remember a lot of what she had in storage, and that meant it was time to toss it.

Those signature saddles in the living room were in the tack room in her longtime home. She still uses them, pulling one down from its bracket when she needs it, tossing it back when she returns. This native Texan keeps her horse in the country, about an hour and a half away from Houston.

These saddles were so beautiful and said so much about her, I knew I had to incorporate them into the design. Other Western touches so subtle they easily go unnoticed include an iron rope motif under the glass of the cocktail table, little cowhide shades with leather stitching on the chandelier, and a hand-rubbed finish on the kitchen cabinets reminiscent of aged barn wood.

The owner did not visit the condo during the remodeling and decorating. "I cried when I walked in here," she said. "I couldn't believe it had so much of my personality. It really tells a story"—her story.

9 Confidence and Connections

SAYING YES

above : Here I am at age 23 with my first long-distance project in Boston.
opposite: To counteract the chilly, snowy view outside the Providence, R.I., apartment in winter, I gave the living room a warm toasty ambience with terra-cotta walls and furnishings in other warm colors. I wanted the color scheme to give the feeling that "the fireplace is burning" even though there was no fireplace.

INEVITABLY I am asked, "How do you get these jobs in places like Hawaii, Acapulco, and Kiev?" While part of the answer sounds like clichés— "…being in the right place at the right time" and "one job leads to another"—the other part is simply that I have been open to saying, "Yes, I can do that."

Like the job in Boston.

Early in my career, in about 1975, I got a call from a real estate developer in Boston. He had been in Houston and had seen this very simple, small apartment complex I had just remodeled, and he thought it was terrific. He said no one in Boston was doing anything like I had done with these apartments. What he saw was my concept of using interior design to merchandise real estate renovations, and it was a little different. But I figured he was going to ask where I bought a light fixture or something like that.

What the developer said next surprised me. I was only 23 years old at the time, had hardly ever traveled, and was just getting started in the business. I remember that he said something like, "We've just bought a project here in Boston, and I'd like for you to come and look at it. Could you come tomorrow?"

"Sure," I replied, sounding a lot more confident than I actually felt. "I can work in Boston."

A few days later, I flew to Boston, where the developer checked me into the best hotel and took me to see the project he and his brother had recently purchased. The place was huge, a virtual city. It featured four gigantic high-rise towers with 465 apartments as well as lobbies, hallways, parking garages, medical offices, and retail spaces—all in downtown Boston. The project had gone into bankruptcy, and that's when they bought it. The developer got lost three times trying to show me the swimming pool; he just couldn't find it.

When the developers asked me if the scope of the project bothered me, I said, "No," again more confidently than I actually felt. They wanted me to be in charge of every visual aspect and tie it all together in an overall marketing theme.

They admitted that other designers they had interviewed seemed overwhelmed. So I took a different tack. Rather than discussing my design ideas, I asked about their business plans. How much had the property cost them? How much did they plan to spend to renovate it? How

long did they intend to keep the property?—all information I needed before I could make any remodeling and decorating plans. They liked my businesslike approach, and, on the spot, said I was the man for the job.

Then, it was time to talk about money. My wife and I were about to buy our first house. To a 23-year-old kid from a small town in Texas, the cost of that two-story house in a nice Houston neighborhood was the most money I could imagine. Also, I had no idea how I would do this project from Houston. I needed to know how often I would have to fly to Boston, where I would stay, how long it would take—all of that. So I quoted them a fee that would be twice the cost of the house. They went berserk and said that was ridiculous. So the negotiating began.

After a lot of give and take, I wound up with a project office in Boston, a secretary, a draftsman, and travel expenses all paid by the developer, plus a fee equal to the cost of my house. The project turned into a big winner for the owners, staying fully rented for 15 years. Then they converted it to condos and made a hefty profit on each unit.

It's amazing how the addition of black awnings gives a crisp, chic look to the exterior of Center Place, an urban apartment community in downtown Providence, Rhode Island. The enormous building seems to rise out of the trees, looking over the park-like setting and the lonely benches.

Besides being the first big out-of-town job for me, the Boston job provided an important connection. The owners hired a young man, who had just gotten an MBA, to do the property management. We became close friends, and, ultimately, he became a developer and the source of all my East Coast work. I'm currently doing houses for him in Palm Beach and Newport as well as seven apartment communities. And it all goes back to that first call almost 30 years ago, when I boldly said, "Sure, I can work in Boston."

THE JAR

Through my East Coast connection—my MBA-developer friend—I got a job working for the Harvard Trust, the Harvard University endowment that owns a considerable amount of real estate. The Trust had a high-rise development called Center Place in Providence, Rhode Island, that was not doing very well financially. Like the complex in Boston, it needed somebody to work some interior design magic. The Trust hired my Boston client, the management/marketing specialist, and he brought me in to merchandise it. They asked me to do a model apartment that would appeal to young, urban professionals.

I wanted the Center Place model apartment to have an inviting, urban look. Once in place, the huge olive oil jug, known as "The Jar," proved to be worth all the drama surrounding its installation.

The first time I walked into the unfinished model apartment, it was 15 degrees outside and everything was covered in snow. I looked out the window at the absolutely gorgeous, white marble, Beaux Arts-style state capitol building and thought "Brrrrr." I decided the color scheme had to say: "the fireplace is burning" even though there was no fireplace in the apartment. So I worked with one of my least favorite colors, orange, in order to create that feeling of warmth. For a twist on an urban look, I softened the contemporary furnishings with ethnic textiles and East Indian artifacts, including a piece that came to be known as "The Jar."

The Jar was this big, tall, crusty, wonderful olive oil jar. Supposedly, it had been ballast in a ship that had sunk in a harbor in India and stayed there for a hundred years. It was covered with barnacles and was the most fabulous jar I'd ever seen. Actually, as big, important pieces of furniture and art go, it wasn't particularly expensive, but the packing and shipping were another story. The Jar became the focal point of my decorating scheme for the model.

On installation day, I got this uneasy feeling when The Jar arrived in a crate that took up most of the elevator. The Jar was looking mighty big. We started uncrating it in the hallway, and the movers—and everybody else involved—kept looking at The Jar, then looking at the door. The movers said they didn't think it would go through the door, but I replied, "Of course it will.'"

It wouldn't.

The Jar was about six inches wider than the door jam. Everyone said it just wasn't going to go through the door, but I was determined, like a mathematician trying to find a solution. I even toyed with ideas like "if I rubbed ice on it, would it shrink?" I racked my brain.

I went downstairs to the lobby, and the British concierge said, "Mr. Stubbs, I understand you are having cauldron problems."

"You mean The Jar?" I asked, and the concierge replied, "Yes, your cauldron." Something about referring to The Jar as a "cauldron" amused me.

I found the building engineer and together we went back upstairs. I suggested we take the door off its hinges, but he said it still wouldn't fit. We tried it anyway, and he was right. So I asked him to take the door frame off. He didn't want to, but he did it, reluctantly. Then we were down to the bare sheetrock and the little metal studs that held it in place.

The movers said it still wouldn't go through, but I insisted that we try. They placed The Jar in the doorway, and I just started pushing it and hitting it, while the building engineer and the movers stood to the side staring at me. Finally, I shoved it through the door, but the door opening had taken the shape of The Jar. The metal studs were bent, and the sheetrock caved in. But The Jar was inside the apartment. Miraculously, when the engineer put the frame back on, it concealed the new jar-shaped curves in the doorway.

All I could think was that some day, some people would try to move The Jar out. They would say: "They got this thing in here; there must be a way to get it out." For me, The Jar was like a permanent fixture. Love the apartment, love The Jar.

opposite: In the bedroom, dark colors on the walls, in the furniture, and in the bed-covering give a cocoon-like feeling to the otherwise ordinary room. I combined a liberal dose of strong colors and subtle patterns to create visual interest and what I call "a moment of luxury".

CANNES

above: My yearly experience at the Cannes Film Festival never ceases to be a surprising and exciting pleasure. My friend and one of my hosts, Staffan Ahrenberg, left, provides entrée to many glamorous events.
opposite: I never really expected to find myself stepping onto the red carpet at Cannes. Here I'm entering the showing of Roman Polanski's *The Piano* with filmmaker Andrew Mysko and his lovely friend, Kate O'Neill.

The ultimate dream for any movie buff is hanging out at the Cannes Film Festival, and for me—a movie aficionado—it has become a yearly reality. My host is my Ukrainian friend and client who generously includes me. Also included in our group is a lovely couple who are well connected in the film community on the producing and financing side. He is a person who seems to know everyone at the Festival.

At Cannes, I have actually had the experience of arriving in a limousine, getting out with all the flash bulbs popping, and walking on the red carpet. The first time I went to the Festival, I assumed I would be on the other side of the ropes looking on, but amazingly, there I was, inside the rope.

At night, we would unwind at Hotel du Cap, a place where you must be on the "A List" just to get in. There I would be in this tiny, crowded bar with such celebrities as Diane Sawyer and Mike Nichols, Elizabeth Hurley, Naomi Campbell, Roman Polanski, Cuba Gooding, Jr., and John Goodman. I must confess to feeling a little star-struck and tongue-tied.

We would sit at a corner table, and, to my surprise, all these people—these stars—would come over to introduce themselves. I hadn't understood the whole structure of the Cannes Film Festival. I had always romanticized the Festival as this wonderful happening, but it's really just a trade convention. People in the film industry "work it," not unlike the way suppliers work a builders' convention where reps from plate glass to plumbing all mingle, selling their wares. At Cannes, it's the stars' job to sell their new films. My hosts are producers and money people, so, in this venue, they really are the top of the food chain, while the more publicly known stars are down a link or two.

Even if I didn't get to meet so many stars, the villa where I stay each time makes the trip worthwhile. I vividly recall the first time I arrived. I drove through the gates that open automatically, passed cypress trees lining each side of the drive, and then I saw the swimming pool, the tennis court, and this classic French villa. The house itself was a big, square box with French doors, all of them open, with white draperies blowing in the breeze, and the Mediterranean Sea behind it. It was an incredible sight.

At sunset, when the lights of Nice were starting to twinkle in the distance, the guests drifted out from the seven bedrooms, dressed in formal attire. They were all in the film industry, and I knew no one except my hosts. Caviar was heaped in silver bowls, and champagne was being passed around. An Andrea Bocelli CD was playing this heavenly music in the background, and I thought, "Just kill me now! Life is never going to get any better than this."

A few years later, when I arrived at the villa again, the first person I encountered was a man with a shaved head and a muscle-bound body like Arnold Schwarzenegger, wearing nothing but a skimpy Speedo bathing suit. I didn't know what to say or where to look. He was coming from the pool, soaking wet, and he shook my hand and mumbled something in this very guttural-sounding language.

As I walked away, I thought, "We won't be friends." That was a sign of my own insecurities, seeing somebody who looks that good in a swim suit. I have reached an age and weight that would make it highly inappropriate for me to be seen in a swim suit.

His name was Slava, and my first impression was wrong. Despite the Speedo, which he always seemed to be wearing, he would become a very important friend for me — and an equally important business connection.

Slava, who is a Ukrainian restaurateur and developer from Kiev, actually spoke English rather well, although I had difficulty understanding him at first. He was usually smoking a cigar and talking on his cell phone. Slowly, however I got to know Slava, and his wife, Oksana, and grew to like them very much.

He asked me what I did and how I knew our hosts — everyone wanted to know everyone else's connection — and I told him I was an interior designer. He asked if I had brought pictures of my work with me. I thought he was just being gracious; I really didn't think he wanted to look at pictures of interiors. But the next morning he asked again. So I brought down my portfolio, and he looked at the pictures quite intently, studying every detail.

"This is very nice," he said. "You are very good. I have a friend in Moscow. He has apartment. He will use you."

All the while, I was thinking, what are the chances of this working out?

A little later by the pool, I was eating breakfast and Slava was walking around in his Speedo, smoking his cigar, and talking in Russian on his cell phone. Every now and then, I would hear him say "Beell Stubbs," although the first time I didn't realize he was saying my name. Of course, I wondered what he was saying and to whom.

When his phone conversation ended, Slava came over and told me he was talking to his friend in Moscow, telling him to hire me to decorate his apartment. Again, I had my doubts about all this, but, amazingly, when I returned to Houston after the Festival, the initial deposit was in my account for a new project in Moscow.

It turned out that about a year before I met Slava at the villa in France, the builder and architect I had worked with in Kiev had asked me to be part of a proposal to design an apartment in Moscow. They put the proposal together and submitted it, but I never heard another word, and had sort of forgotten about it.

That proposal was for Slava's friend. When Slava called him and recommended "Beell Stubbs," the friend remembered, everything clicked, and the project came to life.

When I got home and learned the money had been transferred to my account to seal the deal, I called the architect, who is also my translator, in Kiev. He said it was all because of Slava. I quickly learned that Slava was more than a guy in a Speedo, more than a Kiev restaurateur. He puts people together. He's a great connection and, now, a friend.

opposite: Villa Bacon, my charming home-away-from-home during the Cannes Film Festival, fulfills all my dreams of what a Mediterranean villa should be. *below*: The view across the Mediterranean Sea from Villa Bacon is of Cap d'Antibes. Of all the places I've ever stayed, this villa is one of the most beautiful. Best of all, it's always filled with interesting guests.

Epilogue

IT WAS MORE OF A NIGHTMARE

SO I WAS off to Russia to meet the mystery man who had decided I was the one to design his apartment, all on the recommendation of my new friend, Slava. I spent 24 hours getting to Moscow, and the meeting lasted 45 minutes, just long enough for the new, 37-year-old client to tell me what he wanted in the apartment.

The meeting would have been shorter, but the client didn't speak English, and my translator, the architect, speaks Ukrainian, not Russian. The builder spoke Ukrainian and Russian, not English. Russian and Ukrainian are like Portuguese and Spanish—we think they are virtually the same, but they are not. The architect would translate what I said to the builder who would then translate it to my client. My client would respond, and the process would be reversed. This went around and around until we finally got everything settled.

After the client departed, the architect, the builder, and I toured the raw apartment space. Then I was handed a blueprint and put on an airplane for Houston.

About six weeks later, as I was preparing to leave with my mother, daughter, and son for our annual vacation with my sister in California, the telephone rang. It was the architect in Kiev. He said our Moscow client wanted to see me on Thursday. I told him I was about to go on vacation, and that there were no interior design emergencies at the moment. But the architect insisted. Since it would be only the second meeting for the team, they were very nervous and insisted that I had to be there.

Going to Moscow from the United States is a real hassle because each time you go there, you need a visa that can be secured only from the embassy in Washington or the consulate in New York, together with various other documents—and it takes weeks, not days or hours, to get them. Eventually, if you go to Russia often enough, you can qualify for a multi-entry, year-long visa, but I wasn't eligible at this time.

Then, as if things weren't difficult enough already, the architect said, "By the way, you will need an AIDS test. It's a new requirement to enter the former Soviet Union."

So now I had to interrupt the family vacation, get a visa, an AIDS test (with results), and be in Moscow in three days.

At the bridge and turn of the Moscow River, the sunset shows off the silhouette of the Hotel Ukraina, one of Stalin's sky-scrapers, sometimes referred to as the "seven sisters."

Obviously, I needed to short-circuit this process. I called the executive offices at Houston–based Continental Airlines and asked, "If the head of Continental Airlines had to be in Moscow this week, how would you get him a visa?" They told me about a visa service in New York City that sounded perfect.

All the way to California, I worried about the rush trip to Moscow. By the time we landed, I had decided to attempt to get a quick AIDS test in California. I really didn't want to involve my family, especially my mother, in all of this, but that proved impossible. Once everyone understood what was going on, they all joined the search for a fast AIDS test. Finally, we found a 24-hour test service in Los Angeles, not Newport Beach, where we were headed. That meant we had to alter our plans, so I bribed them with a night in a big, gorgeous suite at the Four Seasons Hotel in Beverly Hills. Then I had to leave a day early to fly back to Houston to prepare for my trip. If I had had any inkling of what lay ahead, I would have savored that night in the luxurious comfort of a Four Seasons bed twice as much as I did.

I landed in Houston about 11 o'clock at night, went by my office to pick up the materials I needed for the meeting, and headed home. I planned to catch a few hours of sleep before I had to leave for the airport at 4 AM to fly to New York to pick up my visa.

When I opened my back door, I stepped into water. My townhouse was flooded. When it rains really hard from a certain direction—and obviously it had—water seeps under my patio doors. It happens about every three years. My beautiful rugs were soaked and ruined. By that time it was almost 2 AM, and I was trying to drag these terribly heavy, wet rugs outside. In the end, I just piled them up in the driveway, packed, and went back to the airport.

When we landed, I took a cab from Newark Airport to Manhattan, picked up my visa, which was all in Russian, and went straight back to the airport to catch a 6 PM flight to Paris. The four-hour layover in Paris seemed endless, but finally we landed in Moscow. I was the first person off the plane and hurried to passport control. I handed over my visa and passport—and this is very typical in Russia—they looked very coldly at me and at the visa, typed something into the computer, and looked back at me. Then, they informed me that my visa had the wrong date and was not valid, and that I should sit down and wait for further directions.

I knew there was a driver waiting for me at the airport and still other people would be waiting at the meeting, so I tried to call them on my European cell phone, but I couldn't get it to work. I tried every possible way to dial, but no luck.

The head of immigration arrived to tell me, again, that my visa was invalid, but for a price, I could get a new one at the consulate at the airport. Two armed guards escorted me to the airport bank to change dollars into rubles, then escorted me back to the little holding area. Sitting there when I returned from the bank were two other people who looked like businessmen.

I had not had anything to drink or been to the restroom since landing three hours earlier. Since I was in a guarded holding area, I left my hand luggage on the chair and went to the restroom, which was just a few feet away. When I returned, my luggage, presentation materials, cell phones, and laptop computer were gone. So were the two men who had been sitting near me.

I rushed into a nearby office, desperate for help. As the officials inside raged at me because the office was off-limits to passengers, I looked out and spotted the two men working their way through the winding maze in the immigration and customs area with my luggage.

"Those two men…," I shouted, "they have my baggage!" I took off after them.

Instead of believing I was a victim, the Russians decided I was a flight risk. The customs and immigration people pulled their guns, assuming, I guess, that I was trying to break into Russia illegally. Now, how often do you think that happens?

The instant I caught up with the two men, they dropped my bags and fled. Fortunately, I got everything back. Plus, I got something extra—two armed guards intent on preventing me from getting any wild ideas about slipping into Russia.

I had no choice but to sit and wait. I was getting cranky, and I had never been so tired. Asking questions got me nowhere. Finally, after about seven hours, another escort came for me. I thought they were going to tell me how much to pay and then let me go.

We walked into the bowels of the airport, and through a maze of back alleyways. It crossed my mind that they might shoot me. At this point, I was not my normal, fearless self. I was exhausted and feeling very uneasy about this situation. We walked past the place where baggage arrives and other behind-the-scenes service areas and stopped at a cramped, circular staircase. We climbed the stairs and were suddenly at an Air France departure gate. A plane was waiting.

"What are we doing here?" I asked.

"Deportation," my escort answered. I suspected it was one of maybe five English words he knew.

"Hello! What? You're deporting me? This cannot be happening," I thought. I was in shock.

I was escorted onto the plane, and, fortunately, to a seat in first class. I had no passport and no tickets. I had handed them over at passport control and they had not been returned. I sank into that first class seat and thought, "I am shaking the dust of Russia off my feet and never going back. There isn't anything that could get me back to this country. I'm going to forget this ever happened."

My anxiety and exhaustion quickly gave in to sleep.

The next thing I remember was that the flight attendant was patting my shoulder. "Monsieur Stubbs," she said, as I began to wake up.

"Monsieur Stubbs, you have business with zee pilot. Please remain in your seat."

And now we're back where we started at the beginning of this memoir. I promised I would tell you what happened, but you probably won't believe it. Trust me; it's all true. OK, I was back in Paris, having slept throughout the four-and-a-half hour flight from Moscow, but I was still exhausted and upset. I wasn't sure if I was dreaming or this was really happening. Eager to get off the plane, I began to gather up my possessions, but the flight attendant reminded me to stay in my seat.

I saw that it would be easier to simply do what I was told, so I sat back down. Everyone else got off, and then the crew arrived to clean up. Next the two French policemen entered the plane, and I realized, to my amazement, that I was being arrested. The pilot appeared with an official-looking envelope. The police signed for it, then escorted me off the plane and into the police station in Charles de Gaulle Airport.

I remember thinking, "Is this one long, bad day or a bad week, or what?" The last time I had had a good night's sleep was at the Four Seasons Hotel in Beverly Hills. Now I was in a French police station. I didn't say a word. It seemed as though I had lost my ability to speak. What would I have said, anyway? If you get deported from Russia, you're either a murderer or a drug dealer. I was neither one, but I had been deported, so what could I have said?

So I sat, silently, in the little police detention room for more than two hours. About 3 AM a person appeared who returned my passport to me, and said something in French, which could easily have been: "Report to prison." I didn't understand him, but I stood up, collected my baggage, and left. Nobody stopped me.

The airport was almost empty, and the floors were being polished as I headed for the information desk, dragging my baggage behind me.

"I need a hotel that has as many stars as possible and is as close as possible," I said to the person at the desk. At that point, I just couldn't face a bad hotel.

She sent me to a new, four-star business hotel inside the airport. It was built in the shape of a ship, so you felt eerily like you were deep inside a boat. To shut out the sound of the airport, they used insulated windows, so when you were in the four-story lobby, you heard a kind of shhhhhhhhh sound. I thought I was having an out-of-body experience or that I had entered the twilight zone.

It had been about 12 hours since I first had been detained at the Moscow airport, so my overriding concern was contacting my new Russian client and the others scheduled to attend the meeting. I didn't know if they knew I had come and gone, if they were still waiting for me at the airport, or what. I couldn't wait to get into a hotel room and make a phone call.

I walked into this beautiful hotel room, and I was really conflicted. I needed to eat, sleep, bathe, remove my contact lenses, and make that phone call—all at the same time. The room had phones by the window, on the desk, on either side of the bed, and by the toilet. I started running the water for a bath, called room service, and began dialing Moscow. I kept getting the same busy signal I had gotten all day on my cell phone. I tried every phone in the room.

Finally, I called the front desk and was assured that I should be able to dial Moscow from my room. So I dialed and dialed and dialed the phone by the toilet. Finally, totally aggravated, I slammed the receiver against the marble wall. Little pieces of plastic flew everywhere, and wires dangled out of the receiver. I was frantic.

I called the front desk again. This time I was told, "Oh, monsieur, we're sorry, the phone system is not working. Could you come down to the front desk and make your call?" After saying something to the desk person about how one has to make calls from the front desk only in one-star hotels, I dressed and went downstairs.

I then tried to call from the hotel's front desk, but I couldn't get through. I tried from the concierge desk. That didn't work, either. I ended up literally lying on my back behind a computer, using a black, rotary-dial emergency phone. I was down on the floor with the dust bunnies when I finally reached the architect/translator in Russia.

"Where are you?" he asked.

"Bad news," I said. "I'm in France."

"Was your flight canceled?" he responded.

"No, I have been to Moscow. I was deported."

"You were what? Deported?" Then he said he would call the client and call me right back.

Within 15 minutes, the architect called back. He said they were truly sorry about my trouble, and could I go to the Russian embassy in Paris in the morning, get another visa, and return on the next flight to Moscow?

"OK," I answered, faintly.

At that point it was 6 AM on the third day of the most frustrating time I have ever had in my career. Thinking there was no way I could bear dealing with the Russian embassy, I again called Continental Airlines in Houston and asked, "If your CEO was in Paris and needed a visa in a hurry, where would he go?" The answer was Express Visa, a service in Paris. It sounded good.

I called Express Visa and said, "I'm at the Paris airport, and I need a visa to go to Moscow today. Can you do that?"

"No problem," I was told. All I needed was my passport and my insurance policy.

I remember the shock wave.

"What?" I asked. "What insurance policy?" No one had ever mentioned anything about needing an insurance policy.

"You have to have an insurance policy to prove you can provide medical insurance when you're in the former Soviet Union," the lady at Express Visa explained. "Bring your visa application, your passport, and your insurance policy to us by two this afternoon, and we can have the visa ready by four o'clock."

I told her I had my health insurance card, but she insisted it had to be a special policy that covers you in the former Soviet Union. Then, she told me the name of a company to call for the policy.

Although I desperately needed sleep, I called the insurance company. I reached a recording—in French, of course—that gave some choices: "*un, deux, trois.*"

I pressed "*un,*" which gave me another message in French that I didn't understand and choices of "*un, deux, trois.*" Finally, I reached a person who explained that they could give a policy to a British citizen, but as an American, I needed to have an American company issue the policy.

By now, it was late morning in Paris. I started calling the United States, where it was the middle of the night. After many fruitless attempts, I contacted a person who suggested I go online and print out the policy from a particular website. I rushed down to the hotel business center, went onto the Internet, found the website, and printed out the policy. Finally, something had worked.

Now I had my insurance policy, my passport, and my visa application form. I checked out of the hotel and took the train into the city. I got a taxi and showed the driver the address of Express Visa. He took me to that address and let me out.

It was the wrong building. After walking for blocks, pulling my luggage behind me, I found

Express Visa. The address had changed. I went inside and said, "Here are my insurance policy, my passport, and my completed visa application."

The person behind the desk looked at my documents, and said, "Oh, monsieur, you are not British."

"Why would that matter?" I asked.

She answered, "Oh, well, only the British need the insurance policy." I felt like shooting somebody—maybe even myself.

I can laugh about it now, but I didn't feel very amused at the time. I wadded up the insurance policy and said, "All right, here are my passport and visa application. Can you get me a visa?"

She told me I had to pay first, in euros. I didn't have enough euros, and asked if they would take a credit card. The answer—naturally—was no. I asked where I could find an ATM, and learned there was one just outside the door on the street.

I went outside to the ATM, put my card in, and a notice appeared that said "Out of service" in French. And my card didn't come back. I started beating on the ATM machine. Suddenly, it started to rain. In fact, it poured—the sky just opened up. When I finally obtained the necessary euros at a different ATM with another credit card and returned, soaking wet, to Express Visa, the woman at the desk said, "I'm sorry, the man has already come from the embassy today. Can you come back tomorrow?"

I was like a wet dog, dragging my luggage behind me. I didn't even argue. I went back to the airport hotel—I didn't have the energy to find another place—and finally got a night's sleep. That helped.

The next day, I returned to Express Visa, and presented my passport and visa application, thinking I was now all set.

"Monsieur, where is your invitation?" the Express Visa lady asked.

"Invitation! You never mentioned an invitation," I said, frustrated beyond belief.

"Oh, monsieur," she replied. "to get a visa for Moscow, you have to have an invitation."

"Where would that invitation come from?" I asked, bewildered.

"Oh, your hotel in Moscow can do an invitation," she said.

By this time, I had learned how to use my European cell phone, so I called the architect/translator in Moscow about the invitation situation. I vaguely remembered having to have an invitation to get the original visa. The reason the person at Express Visa did not mention the invitation when I first called was because she thought I was British. The Brits need medical insurance, but not an invitation, to visit Russia.

The architect arranged for the Marriott Hotel in Moscow to fax an invitation to me in Paris. I was promised a visa at 11 AM the next day. When I arrived, just a little late, there was a sign on the door that said, "Closed for lunch." I could see staff members inside, so I started screaming, "You have to open this door!" They let me in, but they were not happy about it.

I asked for my visa, and she said, "Oh, monsieur, I'm sorry. You don't have enough pages

opposite: The 200-ton Tsar Bell is the largest in the world and rests at the base of the Ivan the Great Bell Tower.
below: Within the Kremlin walls is a historic wealth of architecture and culture, including this lovely church, Assumption Cathedral, with golden onion domes, as seen through snow-covered branches.

139

in your passport for a visa. Would you go to the American Embassy and get more pages?"

I opened my passport and found several empty pages, but the Express Visa lady said that the Russians only accept pages that say "Visa" at the top, and these pages didn't say that.

Next stop, the American embassy. A sign in French and English listed the times the office was open for various services, like 9:30 AM to 10:30 AM for visas and 9:45 AM to 2 PM on Tuesdays and Fridays for extra pages. I was about an hour early, so I ate at a little café nearby.

When I returned to the embassy, I was afraid I would be told to come back in a week or they would mail the pages to me. Instead, they quickly added the pages to my passport. I headed back, once again, to Express Visa.

I handed everything to the Express Visa lady at 2 PM, and, incredibly, my visa was ready by 4 PM. By that time, however, it was too late to make that day's flight to Moscow, so I went back to the hotel.

During all the visa problems in Paris, I also had been trying to locate a wayward package of audio/visual equipment. FedEx had delivered it to my home in Houston, but I had overlooked it when I had arrived to find the flood in my townhouse. Someone from my office retrieved it, and sent it via Continental Airlines to be hand-delivered to me at the airport hotel in Paris. When it did not arrive, I went to the Continental desk. They said to check at the freight area, which required a taxi ride.

Parisian taxi drivers can be rude, and if you get one who has waited three hours in a queue to pick up a fare he assumes is going into Paris, and you tell him that you want to go to another building at the airport, he will go absolutely berserk. In this case, the driver physically pulled me out of his taxi and sent me to the next one in line. That guy sent me back to the first driver, and then the two drivers got into a fist fight. When I finally got a driver to take me to the other side of the airport, he was so angry, I was sure he was trying to kill me by the way he was driving.

Still, the driver did take me to the warehouse area, but we could not find the place for Continental. I went back and forth about four times. Finally, I found an unmarked door that led to the little Continental office in a cavernous warehouse. But no package. To this day, we haven't found it. I thought I was going to have a heart attack trying to find that package.

Finally, I made it to Moscow and the long-delayed meeting. From the time I left Beverly Hills until I finally got into Moscow—legally—five days had passed. Although I did finally get a few nights of sleep, it was the worst trip I have ever taken.

The meeting lasted only 45 minutes. When I apologized for not being there when it was originally scheduled, my new client's response actually energized me.

"Projects that start off with difficulties usually have great results," he said. "The trouble is behind us. Let's move forward."

And suddenly, Russia was looking good again.

This is a haggard version of me at Sheremetyero Airport after 24 hours of travel and 12 hours of meetings. The smile is because I am leaving.

CREDITS

COVER
PHOTOGRAPHY: Heinz Kugler
MAKEUP: Veronica Martinez
STYLIST: Courtney Stubbs
BACKGROUND FABRIC: Robert Allen
ENDPAPER FABRIC: Beacon Hill

PROLOGUE
PHOTOGRAPHY: Heinz Kugler

CHAPTER 1: THE HOUSTON PENTHOUSE
PRINCIPAL PHOTOGRAPHY: E. Joseph Deering
ADDITIONAL INTERIOR DESIGN: Trisha Dodson
ADDITIONAL INTERIOR DESIGN: Dian Diamond
CONTRACTOR: Sam Marshall, Jr.
FURNISHINGS: Ernest Jaster Custom Designs
DRAPERIES: Heines Custom Draperies

CHAPTER 2: THE UKRANIAN COTTAGE
PRINCIPAL PHOTOGRAPHY: Phillip H. Ennis
GENERAL CONTRACTOR: Volodymyr Aveskoulov, Vil Construction
ARCHITECT/PROJECT MANAGER: Roman Shwed, AIA
LIGHTING DESIGN: Carl Mitchell, Aspen Lighting Designs
ILLUSTRATOR: James Hogg
DRAPERIES: Gary Archer, Gulf Drapery
FABRICS: Leggetts

CHAPTER 3: THE DACHA
PRINCIPAL PHOTOGRAPHY: Phillip H. Ennis
ADDITIONAL INTERIOR DESIGN: Dawn Frazier
GENERAL CONTRACTOR: Volodymyr Aveskoulov, Vil Construction
ARCHITECT/PROJECT MANAGER: Roman Shwed, AIA
LIGHTING DESIGN: Carl Mitchell, Aspen Lighting Designs
THEATER DESIGN: Theo Kalomirakis
AUDIO VIDEO INSTALLATION: Robert Eitel, Robert's Home Audio & Video
ILLUSTRATOR: James Hogg
DRAPERIES: Gary Archer, Gulf Drapery
FABRICS: Brunschwig & Fils, Nancy Corzine, Old World Weavers,
    Pindler & Pindler, Robert Allen, Beacon Hill, Scalamandré,
    Schumacher, Stroheim Romann

CHAPTER 4: A VILLA IN ACAPULCO
PRINCIPAL PHOTOGRAPHY: Rob Muir
ADDITIONAL INTERIOR DESIGN: Dian Diamond
GENERAL CONTRACTOR: Raul Figurola
ARCHITECT: Brit Perkins, AIA, EDI
ADDITIONAL ARCHITECTURE: Marcelo Del Rio
PROJECT MANAGER: Claudia Landis
LANDSCAPE DESIGN: Ben Lednicky, Ben Lednicky & Associates

CHAPTER 5: A NEWPORT SCHOOLHOUSE
PHOTOGRAPHY: Aaron Usher, III
CONTRACTOR: O. Ahlborg & Sons
ARCHITECT: Michael Abbott, AIA, The Newport Collaborative
DEVELOPER: Gatehouse Group
BRANDING: Paul Beaulieu, Media Concepts

CHAPTER 6: LONDON SURPRISES
PHOTOGRAPHY: Heike Bohnstengel
INTERIOR DESIGN: Tyler London Ltd.
ARCHITECT: Tyler London Ltd.
DEVELOPER: Tyler London Ltd.
LIGHTING DESIGN: Absolute Action
FABRICS: Donghia, Kravet

CHAPTER 7: KONA, HAWAII
PHOTOGRAPHY: Rob Muir
ADDITIONAL INTERIOR DESIGN: Dawn Frazier
GENERAL CONTRACTOR: Robin Ledson, Ledson Construction
LIGHTING DESIGN: Tim Bailey, Lighting Inc.
FURNISHINGS: Lynn Yellen, Washington Park Design Center (LADCO)
DRAPERIES: G&S Custom Draperies
FABRICS: Robert Allen, Beacon Hill, Schumacher, Summer Hill

CHAPTER 8: AN AMERICAN TRIO
Ranch-Style Revise
PHOTOGRAPHY: Rob Muir
ADDITIONAL INTERIOR DESIGN: Dawn Frazier
GENERAL CONTRACTOR: R. A. Briggs, Briggs Construction & Co.
KITCHEN DESIGN: Keith Davis, Davis Kitchen Designs
LIGHTING DESIGN: Tim Bailey, Lighting, Inc.
FURNISHINGS: Lynn Yellen, Washington Park Design Center (LADCO)
DRAPERIES: G&S Custom Draperies
FABRICS: Kravet, Pindler & Pindler

California Dreaming
PHOTOGRAPHY: Rob Muir
GENERAL CONTRACTOR: Paul McEachern, McEachern Co., Inc.
FABRICS: Brunschwig & Fils, Kravet, Robert Allen, Beacon Hill

Urban Cowgirl
PHOTOGRAPHY: Rob Muir
ADDITIONAL INTERIOR DESIGN: Dawn Frazier
GENERAL CONTRACTOR: Gary Trentham, Trentham Contractors
FURNISHINGS: Lynn Yellen, Washington Park Design Center (LADCO)
DRAPERIES: Gary Archer, Gulf Drapery
FABRICS: Pindler & Pindler, Robert Allen, Beacon Hill

CHAPTER 9: CONNECTIONS
Providence, Center Place
PRINCIPAL PHOTOGRAPHY: Chuck Choi
ARCHITECT: Archetype Architecture

EPILOGUE
PHOTOGRAPHY: Author's personal collection

No matter what glamorous or exotic locale I experience, or what excitement I encounter, I am always happiest surrounded by family and friends—just as I am here at my 50th birthday celebration.